THE SIMPLY GREAT II COOKBOOK

THE SIMPLY GREAT II
COOKBOOK
More fine recipes from the kitchens of Chuck Muer

TRIBUTE EDITION

C.A. Muer Corporation

Momentum Books Ltd.
Troy, Michigan

Manufactured in the United States of America

1997   1996   1995   4 3 2 1

Line drawings by Bill Olendorf
Crab designs based on logo by Christian E. Pohl
as modified by Sharon Kelley

Published by Momentum Books Ltd.
6964 Crooks Road, Suite #1
Troy, Michigan 48098 USA

ISBN: 1-879094-38-X

Dedication

*To the friends
of Chuck and Betty Muer*

It has been almost two years since "The Storm of the Century" at which time my parents Chuck and Betty Muer along with their dear friends George and Lynne Drummey were lost at sea. The hope of finding them has faded but their memories still remain bright in the hearts of their friends and family both near and far.

It is ironic to think that only five years ago when my father wrote his first cookbook he was very aware of how dynamic and changing it could become through the years. But never did he dream that one day his friends and family would be involved in publishing a Tribute Edition of the cookbook.

People who knew my father enjoyed his many-facetted personality. He was a perfectionist, but not perfect; he was a man of humor, but had a depth of seriousness to him; liberal, but always conservative; self centered yet never selfish. Chuck Muer lived life on an emotional rollercoaster filled with the highs and lows of a man living a full life with no thoughts of regret.

For all his many interests, he enjoyed simple pleasures most of all. He would wake up very early each day, often just so he could photograph the sunrise. Perhaps his special gift that so endeared him to many people was his knack of making even the most forlorn person feel special and needed. To those of us whose lives he touched with that gift, it will forever be his priceless legacy—the gift of knowing he truly cared about everyone he encountered.

My mother, Betty Jane Muer, was a woman whose entire life was dedicated to the needs of her husband and family. "Betts", as my father used to call her, was a woman of true beauty and class. She was my father's equal and was respected amongst her friends and peers as fiercely loyal and honest lady with a comic wit that could bring anyone to fits of laughter even in the most trying of times.

As I grew older my mother and I became friends and through our friendship I began to understand this woman. Betty battled with the traditional "wife" role, searching for an identity of her own. I am sure living in the shadows of such a dynamic man as Chuck Muer was not easy.

Through her searches my mother discovered that she possessed a true talent for decorating and became a designer. Her first professional project was the designing of "Big Fish" in Dearborn, Michigan. Local critics took notice of her tasteful selection of decor and the atmosphere she created. I will never forget the jubilant smile of victory that filled her face when she read the favorable reviews of her first project.

My memory of my mother and friend, Betty Muer, is one of respect and admiration for a woman who had the courage and drive to make her dreams become a reality.

This book was conceived to give permanence to the thoughtful comments of my parents' friends and business associates who took the time to put to paper their experiences and feelings of lives once lived. On behalf of the Muer family and organization, I want to thank everyone who contributed.

For Chuck and Betty Muer, their friends were their reality check and from them they drew the emotional support that helped them build sense of who they were. This book is dedicated not only to the memory of Chuck and Betty Muer but also to their friends, in gratitude for the richness you brought into their lives.

—Susan Muer

Contents

This book is dedicated to Chuck and Betty Muer who lost their lives on March 13, 1993 in the "Storm of the Century."

Preface

This book was inspired by the memory of Chuck and Betty Muer who lost their lives at sea on March 13, 1993. Chuck Muer was the founder of the C.A. Muer Corporation and for 28 years was its visionary. Today there are twenty restaurants in five states with additional locations scheduled to open in 1995. The company continues to be a leader in the industry as a result of Chuck having charted a clear course and developing a strong team to carry on his work. It is a testament to his leadership and vision that the C. A. Muer Corporation has set high quality food and professional service standards since its conception in 1965, and will be a leading innovator for many years to come.

Chuck Muer often referred to his numerous standards for high quality food and service as "Muerisms". These "Muerisms" are still alive today, and are what set the C. A. Muer collection of restaurants apart from the many others that have tried to duplicate his success.

Chuck Muer was not only a man, but a philosophy, a style and a way of life. Although he may not be with us in the physical sense, he still lives in our restaurants and through the people he touched. We will toast him and to his many accomplishments this year as we celebrate the 30th anniversary of the company that bears his name.

—Susan Muer
C. A. Muer Corporation

Acknowledge-ments

My deepest thanks to the many people who helped with the creation of the "tribute edition". My father's most loyal friend and associate Donna Bauer helped type and edit the new recipes included in this book. And she also gave me the courage to put my own personal tribute on paper.

I would also like to thank Tommy Holland, chef at Charley's Crab, Palm Beach; Chef Peter Ashcraft; Ken Kozma, pastry chef at Charley's Crab, Troy, Michigan; Dorothy Lewis, Pastry chef at Big Fish Too in Madison Heights, Michigan; and Chef Jim Blake, our corporate executive chef, for helping me adapt, test and refine these recipes to work as well in your kitchen as in ours.

I gratefully acknowledge the invaluable contribution of Chef Larry Pagliara and Chef Carmen Vilican. They have also passed on but have left their indelible mark through their recipes and food philosophy. They both shared common threads that together gave our corporation what is today our successful food style...SIMPLY GREAT FOOD!

Lastly, Chuck Muer would have wanted us to thank the many loyal guests who continued to dine with him for the first thirty years and still do so today. Chuck must have told us 10,000 times or more that "the guest is number one." In fact, on the corporate organizational chart the box above the one with Chuck's name was a box that contained the name to whom Chuck reported—"The Guest." He never let us forget it—and we never will.

—Susan Muer

Signature Recipes

The Original Charley's Crab, Pine Lake, Michigan

GAZPACHO SALSA
CAJUN REMOULADE SAUCE
CAJUN SEASONING
HONEY MUSTARD DRESSING
MUSTARD SAUCE
PROVENÇAL SAUCE
BASIC WHITE CLAM SAUCE
CLARIFIED BUTTER
CASINO BUTTER
TARTAR SAUCE
CHEF LARRY'S TARTAR SAUCE
To Shuck an Oyster
To Open Clams
To Clean Mussels
CHARLEY'S CHOWDER
CHEF LARRY'S BLESSING (Olive Oil marinade)
MARTHA'S VINEYARD SALAD
HOUSE BREAD
CAESAR SALAD
RICE PILAF
STUFFED FLOUNDER
CHARLEY'S BUCKET
CRABMEAT STUFFING
LOBSTER LARRY with Crabmeat Stuffing
KEY LIME PIE

I got to know Chuck when he agreed to host the Grand Ole Tashmoo Whistle Blowin' at the River Crab in St. Clair. Each Labor Day, from 1977 to 1982, the whistles of many famous Great Lakes ships were brought to the site to be blown. Young and old alike were able to pull the lever just for fun or to salute a passing freighter. ... Chuck realized the fond memories he brought back to people who remembered those endearing and forgotten sounds, and I realized then how he genuinely loved people.

–Jim Clary
St. Clair, Michigan

This is a great relish for salmon or any white fish. It is also good for a chilled salmon salad.

GAZPACHO SALSA
Recipe by Chef Jim Blake

This recipe is a take-off on our traditional Gazpacho Soup. Great as a relish.

Yield: 4 servings
(16 ounces)

1 cup plum tomatoes, chopped, include juice
1/4 cucumber, diced
3 tablespoons red pepper, diced
3 tablespoons yellow pepper, diced
3 tablespoons green pepper, diced
1 teaspoon scallion, chopped
1 teaspoon garlic, chopped fine
2 teaspoons red onion, diced
1/2 teaspoon jalapeno pepper, diced
1/2 lemon, squeeze & reserve the juice, grate & reserve the zest
1 ounce olive oil
Kosher salt, to taste
Black pepper, fresh-cracked, to taste
1 teaspoon fresh basil

1. Finely dice tomato (saving the juice), cucumber, red pepper, yellow pepper, green pepper, scallion, garlic, red onion, and jalapeno pepper.

2. Combine all ingredients, refrigerate, and let marinate for 1 hour before using.

3. Use 2 ounces per serving *(see Side Note)*.

Signature Recipes

CAJUN REMOULADE SAUCE
Recipe by Chef Peter Ashcraft

Yield: 3 cups

1 1/2 cups Chef Larry's Tartar Sauce (see page 13)
2 scallions (greens only)
1/2 tablespoon Cajun Seasoning (see page 7)
1/2 tablespoon paprika
1/2 fresh lemon, the juice of
1/3 cup fresh ripe tomatoes, seeds removed, finely diced
2 tablespoons celery, finely chopped
2 tablespoons green pepper, finely chopped

1. Place Tartar Sauce and scallion greens in blender and blend until well mixed.

2. Transfer to a bowl and combine with remainder of the ingredients and mix well.

3. Refrigerate for 3 hours to allow the flavors to marinate.

*T*he sprint through life is enhanced by the enthusiasm and gusto that people display at every waking moment in their lifetime. Those qualities were never better exhibited than by Chuck and Betty Muer.

–Nino Ciaravino
Attorney at Law
Harper Woods, Michigan

Betty and Chuck were contributors. They enjoyed life, and people enjoyed life more when they were around. ... How grateful we should be for having had them in our lives. ... [Chuck] lived his faith. ... He was an employer who recognized the interdependence between employees and employers and he wanted to be fair in his policies. Chuck was very interested in education and in school reform. He firmly believed that if people were convinced about the worth of something then they would be able to achieve it, if they were willing to work hard.

–Rev. Msgr. F. Gerald
Martin
St. Paul on the Lake
Grosse Pointe Farms,
Michigan

CAJUN SEASONING
Idea inspired by Paul Prudhomme. Recipe by Chef Rocky

Yield: 1 cup

4 tablespoons paprika
2 tablespoons salt
1 tablespoon garlic powder
1 1/4 tablespoons cayenne pepper
1 tablespoon white pepper
1 tablespoon black pepper
1 1/2 teaspoons dried thyme
1 1/2 teaspoons dried oregano

1. In a bowl mix together all spices.

2. Can be stored in a zip-lock bag for later use.

The spices used here are harsh when uncooked. Any fish with a high oil content, such as bass, bluefish, mackerel salmon, pompano, and lake trout, are well suited for blackening using this recipe. So are beef, pork and chicken. This Cajun Seasoning is also great to use in sauces or just to spice up your life a little bit.

HONEY MUSTARD DRESSING
Recipe by Chef Larry

Yield: 4 to 6 servings

1 cup peanut oil
1/2 cup honey
1 teaspoon garlic, minced
1/4 teaspoon paprika
1 tablespoon fresh ginger root, minced
2 tablespoons fresh lemon juice
3 tablespoons cider vinegar
1/2 cup stone ground mustard

Combine all ingredients in bowl. Whip together well for 3 minutes or until emulsified.

*C*huck led many lives. Sailor. Restaurateur. Father. Husband. Friend. I knew him best as the partner to a little second grade girl at the Cornerstone School on Linwood Avenue. Chuck came to both partner days to do a little project with Jessica Rivers. They made silly hats together. Laughed. She told him about her work and he told her about his. There was no pretense. Just friendship. They exchanged letters. More importantly, they each gave each other a little of their own hearts. Just before Chuck left for Florida for his last great adventure here with us, he left me a message saying he wanted to help recruit more partners for all the kids at Cornerstone when he got back from Florida. That was like Chuck. He was always thinking of helping someone else, even in the midst of his own pursuits. We all should shed such light.

–Clark Durant
Chairman of the Board
Cornerstone Schools
Detroit

I knew Chuck Muer for over thirty years. ... The most important thing that I'll always remember about Chuck was the tremendous amount of confidence he had in life, others, and himself. I can't swim, I hated boats of all kinds, I never sailed, but Chuck convinced me to join him on his sailboat to participate as a crew member in the Key West races in February, just weeks before the tragedy. ... During that trip, he instilled confidence in me as a sailor and, honestly, I enjoyed every minute of those five fabulous days. I'll never forget him.

–William "Willie" Stone
W. S. Insurance Group
West Bloomfield,
Michigan

MUSTARD SAUCE
Recipe by Chef Rocky

Yield: 1 1/2 cups

1 cup mayonnaise
1/4 cup Dijon mustard
1/2 teaspoon dry mustard
2 teaspoons lemon juice

Combine all ingredients in a bowl and blend thoroughly. Sauce may be kept refrigerated in a covered container for up to 2 weeks.

Unlike many mustard sauces, ours is not sweet. It complements any cold seafood.

PROVENÇAL SAUCE
Recipe by Chef Larry

This classic country sauce is intensely flavored with garlic, herbs, tomatoes and olive oil. It is used as a base or a garnish in many of our recipes.

Yield: 3 cups

1/4 cup olive oil
6 cloves garlic, peeled
1/2 cup onion, very finely diced
1/3 cup celery, very finely diced
1/2 teaspoon dried oregano
1/4 cup parsley, very finely chopped
1/2 teaspoon dried basil
10 to 12 whole plum tomatoes, peeled, seeded and chopped into
*   1/4-inch pieces*
1 cup tomato juice (out-of-season substitute 3 cups canned
*   whole tomatoes for tomatoes and juice.)*
3/4 cup dry white table wine
2 tablespoons clam base

1. In a medium-size, stainless steel saucepan, heat olive oil to frying temperature. Add garlic and cook until golden brown. Remove garlic with a slotted spoon and discard.

2. Add onions and celery to the oil. Sauté for 3 minutes until onions are translucent. Add oregano, parsley and basil. Cook over medium heat for 1 minute.

3. Add chopped tomatoes, tomato juice, wine and clam base. If you are using canned tomatoes, use the juice from the can rather than a cup of tomato juice.

4. Bring sauce to a boil, then reduce heat to simmer. Cook for 10 minutes. Skim top of sauce.

5. Cool and skim sauce again. Cover and refrigerate. The sauce has a shelf life of up to 7 days.

Quick Meal
For a healthy and delicious meal, drain freshly cooked pasta, add Provençal Sauce, toss together in a saucepan and warm over low heat for a few minutes. Add a salad with balsamic vinegar and a crusty bread, and you have a feast.

Chuck was a fellow member of the Young Presidents' Organization. You must be president of a company before the age of forty. We had wonderful times at YPO functions around the world, such as: Betty ordered a strange dish in Hong Kong and had trouble chewing it—then realized it was fish in a bag! We missed a big banquet in Singapore because Chuck wanted to eat at a "great" restaurant he had heard about. It turned out to be picnic benches in an open field with god-awful food and dishes washed in a dirty tub. ... We are fortunate to have been their friends ... watching seven children grow ... telling jokes and always laughing.

–Art and Brigitte Geiger
Jupiter, Florida

BASIC WHITE CLAM SAUCE
Recipe by Chef Larry

Yield: 3 cups

2 cups olive oil
2 cloves garlic
3/4 cup hot water
2 tablespoons clam base
1/4 cup fresh parsley, finely chopped

1. Blend garlic and 1 cup olive oil in a blender to emulsify.

2. In a bowl, mix clam base with hot water.

3. In a saucepan, heat remaining 1 cup olive oil to frying temperature and remove from stove.

4. Quickly add blended garlic and oil mixture to hot oil, being careful not to burn the garlic.

5. Mix in chopped parsley.

6. Add clam base mixture to oil.

7. Let cool to room temperature. This sauce may be kept refrigerated for up to 2 weeks.

Variation: 1 1/4 cups of clam juice may be substituted for the water and clam base.

Red Clam Sauce: To make Red Clam Sauce, add an equal amount of Provençal Sauce *(see page 10)* to this White Clam Sauce.

A versatile sauce: Use White Clam Sauce to sauté vegetables, or simply toss with pasta.

CLARIFIED BUTTER

This recipe may be used to make any quantity of Clarified Butter. Make only as much as you need for the recipe you will be using.

1. Melt the butter over low heat.

2. Transfer melted butter to a bowl and allow to cool.

3. Pure butter fat–the Clarified Butter–will rise to the top. Skim off and set aside for cooking. Discard the solids and water that remain in the bowl.

Clarified butter can be made ahead of time and stored in the refrigerator.

CASINO BUTTER
Recipe by Chef Larry

Yield: 2 1/2 cups

1 pound butter or margarine, softened
1/3 cup dry white table wine, room temperature
1/4 teaspoon salt
1/8 teaspoon ground white pepper
1 large garlic clove, minced
1 strip anchovy, finely chopped
2 tablespoons parsley, washed, dried and finely chopped
2 tablespoons green pepper, finely chopped
2 tablespoons pimientos, finely chopped

This recipe can be easily increased or decreased by adjusting given quantities of ingredients.

1. In an electric mixer place softened butter, wine, salt, pep per,garlic and anchovy.Mix until wine and butter are well blended.

2. Stop mixer and add parsley, green pepper and pimientos. Turning mixer on and off, incorporate ingredients and mix until evenly blended

To avoid having the butter turn green, wash the chopped parsley and wring it out in a towel, squeezing out water and color.

3. Cover and refrigerate. This sauce will keep well for up to 2 weeks.

Try either of these tartar sauces as a dip for french fries or crusty breads.

TARTAR SAUCE

This is a variation of a recipe developed by my grandmother, Susan Malburg Muer, for the original Joe Muer's restaurant.

Yield: 2 1/2 cups

2 cups mayonnaise
1/4 cup dill pickle relish, well drained
1/4 cup onions, finely diced
1/4 cup parsley, finely diced

1. Mix all ingredients together.

2. Cover and refrigerate. Tartar Sauce will last for up to 2 weeks.

CHEF LARRY'S TARTAR SAUCE

Yield: 2 cups

This tartar sauce takes on the character of a Remoulade Sauce and is especially good with cold meat, poultry and shellfish.

1 1/2 cups mayonnaise
1 tablespoon onion, very finely diced
3 tablespoons kosher dill pickle, very finely diced
1 stalk celery, very finely diced
1 small garlic clove, minced
1 tablespoon capers, finely chopped
2 teaspoons fresh chives, finely chopped
1 anchovy, minced
1 teaspoon Worcestershire sauce
1 teaspoon lemon juice

1. Combine all ingredients in the order given. Blend well.

2. Cover and refrigerate. Sauce will last for up to 2 weeks.

To Shuck an Oyster:

Most non-professionals find oyster shucking difficult. Just finding the break between the top and bottom shell often requires a trained eye. Although the method described here may not be elegant, it is quite effective and simple enough for novices.

Equipment needed:
Oyster knife or a sturdy paring knife
Flat-blade screwdriver
Stiff brush
Glove or towel

1. Wash the oysters by scrubbing them thoroughly under cold running water with a stiff brush. Discard any oysters that have an odor, that have broken shells, or that do not close tightly when touched.

2. Place the oyster, cupped side down, on a steady surface. Use a glove or towel to protect the hand that steadies the oyster. The hinge of the oyster should face outward toward the hand holding the screwdriver.

3. Set the tip of a clean, flat-blade screwdriver into the hinge (see illustration).

4. Push the screwdriver deep into the seam and twist the blade, breaking the oyster's hinge. Be careful not to insert the screwdriver so far as to damage the oyster meat.

5. The flat top shell should now be loose, with the seam between the shells sufficiently open to insert the oyster or paring knife. Carefully run the knife beneath the oyster along the cupped bottom shell to cut the single muscle that is located about 1/3 of the way in from the tip of the oyster. Loosen the oyster completely from the bottom shell.

If you've made a terrible mess of it and have shell all over, then–but only then–run it under water. This is a last resort as the water will wash away the briny character that oyster lovers look for. Your penalty for messing up this oyster is to eat it on the spot!

6. Flip the oyster over and remove the cupped shell. Then slide the knife under the oyster and cut it away from the flat shell.

7. Before serving check the oyster for shell fragments.

8. Freshly shucked oysters should be served on the flat top shell. This is an indication that the oysters have just been shucked and are likely to be still alive.

We shared many enjoyable moments with Chuck and Betty. They added such sparkle and energy to every occasion.

–Sam and Harriet Lafata
Gourmet House Inc.
St. Clair Shores, Michigan

To Open Clams:

The trick to opening a clam is to leave its meat intact while only cutting the muscles that hold it to its shell. With a little practice, you'll be able to serve clams on the half shell, live and unmarked.

Equipment needed:
  Clam knife
  Stiff brush
  Glove or towel

1. Wash clams by scrubbing the shells thoroughly under cold running water with a stiff brush. Discard any clams that have broken shells or that do not close when touched.

2. Wear a glove or use a towel to protect your hand from the clam shell and the knife. Hold the clam in the palm of your hand with the hinge of the clam pointing along the line of your thumb.

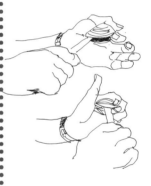

3. At the top edge of the clam, force the blade of the clam knife between the shells. Use the fingers of the hand holding the clam to pull the blade into the clam; pushing with the hand holding the knife is less controllable and usually breaks the shell. (See illustration.)

4. Twist the knife to force a small opening. Insert the tip of your index finger and withdraw the knife.

5. Reinsert the blade on an upward angle following the contour of the top shell. Gently sever the two muscles close to the shell.

6. Twist off the top shell and discard.

7. Free the clam from the bottom shell by severing the muscle from the shell. Again the knife should follow the shell contour and snip the muscle close to the shell.

8. Check for small shell fragments before serving.

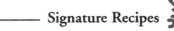

During the hours of many automobile trips to and from Lansing with Chuck to meet with the legislature's leadership "Quadrant" when he was chairman of the Chamber [of Commerce], we developed plans for several chamber initiatives that live today in our community: the chamber's regional economic development program (Business Attraction Council), the traditional Chamber Cruise into the Mackinac Conference, and creation of the Greater Detroit Foreign Trade Zone, just to name a few. Chuck led the chamber into an era of pro-active community leadership.

–Frank E. Smith
President, Greater Detroit
Chamber of Commerce
Detroit

To Clean Mussels:

1. Scrub mussels under cold running water with a stiff brush to remove mud and dirt.

2. Remove the clumps of very strong fibers, the "beard" of the mussel, by pulling or clipping with a scissors.

3. Keep mussels refrigerated until ready to cook and serve.

CHARLEY'S CHOWDER

A restaurant is defined by its signature dishes. Sometimes this just happens. But when we made the decision to open our first Charley's Crab, we also resolved to feature a signature soup and entree. The following morning, Chef Larry sought me out and exclaimed for all to hear in the lobby of the Hotel Pontchartrain, "I've got the soup!" He made it for lunch that day and we finalized it on the spot. Like many of Chef Larry's dishes, this Mediterranean-style fish chowder reflects his Italian heritage.

Yield: 8 servings

1/4 cup olive oil
3 medium garlic cloves, peeled and crushed
1 cup onion, finely diced
1/4 teaspoon basil
1/4 teaspoon oregano
Pinch of thyme
8 to 10 whole plum tomatoes, peeled, seeded and chopped into
    1/4-inch pieces (or 2 cups stewed tomatoes, finely chopped,
    without the juice)
1 cup tomato sauce
6 cups clam juice
1 pound boneless pollack, cut into 1-inch cubes
2 tablespoons fresh parsley, chopped
Salt to taste

1. In a 4-quart soup pot, heat olive oil. Add garlic. When the garlic turns brown, remove it quickly with a slotted spoon and discard. Reduce the heat.

2. Add celery, onions and spices to oil. Cook over medium heat for 5 minutes.

3. Add tomatoes and tomato sauce; simmer for 5 minutes.

*C*huck Muer always reminded me of a Detroit citizen who loved his city and his family. It was clear that education was very important to him, and I was impressed that his sons commuted from St. Clair to the University of Detroit High School in Detroit, where my son also attended. That represented to me quite a statement about "schools of choice." ... His boundless energy in pursuit of alternative schools for our community remains a challenge to us all.

–Walter E. Douglas
President
Avis Ford
Southfield, Michigan

*C*huck and Betty were those rare individuals who made the world better. They saw what could be and had the will and the presence to make it come true.

–John W. Broad
President, Broad, Vogt &
Conant Inc.
River Rouge, Michigan

4. Add clam juice and pollack. Cover and bring to a boil.

5. Remove cover and boil for 10 minutes longer. With a wire whisk, whip soup to break up fish into pea-size flakes.

6. Reduce to a simmer and cook for 20 minutes.

7. Add parsley and salt to taste.

To Serve:
Serve soup hot with House Bread *(see page 22)*.

Type of Fish:
The type of fish used in this soup is crucial. The flavor of the chowder is derived from the amount of oil in the flesh. A firm textured fish with a high oil content is required. Those fish include pollack, bluefish, striped bass, trout and catfish.

Quick Lunch:
While working on these recipes in the restaurants, Chef Rocky would make a quick, satisfying lunch by ladling Charley's Chowder over Rice Primavera in a soup crock. Try this at home with any leftover rice you may have in the refrigerator.

CHEF LARRY'S BLESSING (Olive Oil marinade)

Chef Larry would perform this final act over an already good thing to make it even more wonderful.

Yield: 1 1/4 cups

1 large garlic clove, peeled
1 cup olive oil
2 tablespoons dried oregano
1/8 teaspoon salt

1. In a blender, emulsify garlic and olive oil. Add spices, then turn blender on and off intermittently to mix thoroughly.

2. Store covered at room temperature until ready to use. The marinade will keep for about 1 week.

CROUTONS

Croutons are easy to make and show your personal touch. For this recipe you can use any type of bread you wish.

Yield: 4 cups

1. Spread bread cubes on a baking sheet and drizzle with Chef Larry's Blessing.

2. Toast in a 350 degree oven until golden brown.

3. Cool and store in an airtight container until ready to use.

To emphasize their homemade quality, cut the croutons in irregular shapes and sizes.

Cooking in oil
Olive oil is heated for cooking just as it starts to give off a bluish smoke. In this recipe, it is essential not to burn the garlic. The oil cooking process will require your undivided attention.

Use Larry's Blessing to:
Marinate meats, fish or fowl before grilling, baste grilled vegetables, toss with salad greens and croutons, and brush on breads and pizza crusts.

Garlic Oil
Browning whole garlic cloves in hot oil and then discarding the cloves produces a highly aromatic, flavored oil for cooking.

The Raspberry-Maple Dressing can also be used as a marinade for seafood and poultry. The sugar in the recipe, be it honey or maple syrup, caramelizes and glazes grilled foods.

Roasted walnuts can be used in place of the toasted pine nuts.

To Serve:
Divide lettuce evenly onto 6 chilled plates and top each with the blue cheese, onion rings and toasted pine nuts.

MARTHA'S VINEYARD SALAD
With Raspberry-Maple Dressing
Recipe by Chef Rocky

We originally called this simply "House Salad," but after a few years Betty and I gave it a proper name. We had just ordered the house salad from super server Martha Collins, and the name "Martha's Vineyard" just jumped into our heads. The recipe was inspired by the Machus Salad at Machus Reds Fox, Birmingham, Michigan.

Yield: 6 servings

1 cup white wine vinegar
1 cup red wine vinegar
1/2 cup raspberries (fresh or frozen)
1/2 cup olive oil
1/2 cup vegetable oil
1/2 cup maple syrup
2 tablespoons Dijon mustard
2 tablespoons dried tarragon leaves (or 4 tablespoons fresh)
Dash of salt to taste
1 head Bibb lettuce, washed and dried
1/2 head red leaf lettuce, washed and dried
1/4 cup crumpled blue cheese
12 rings red onion, sliced 1/4-inch thick
3 tablespoons pine nuts, toasted

1. First prepare a raspberry vinegar: combine red and white wine vinegars and raspberries. Cover and let sit 48 hours. Strain the vinegar, and store at room temperature. (You can also use commercial raspberry vinegar, which is available at specialty stores.)

2. To make Raspberry-Maple Dressing, whisk together in a bowl 1/2 cup of the raspberry vinegar, the oils, maple syrup, mustard, tarragon and salt.

3. Tear lettuce leaves by hand and toss in a large bowl with 3/4 cup of dressing.

HOUSE BREAD
Recipe by Chef Larry

Yield: 4 loaves

1 package dry yeast
1 1/2 cups water
1 tablespoon sugar
1 tablespoon salt
2 tablespoons olive oil
4 cups high gluten bread flour
1/4 cup kosher salt
2 tablespoons poppy seed
Chef Larry's Blessing (see page 20)

Special Equipment:
Although the recipe can also be mixed by hand, an electric mixer with paddle attachment or a food processor with plastic dough blade is recommended.

1. In a bowl, sprinkle yeast on top of warm water (110 degrees). When yeast has dissolved and starts to form bubbles, add sugar, salt and oil. Mix well.

2. Using an electric mixer or food processor on low speed, slowly mix in the 4 cups of bread flour. As the ingredients combine, the dough should become soft. If it is sticky, add a little more flour.

3. Knead dough at medium speed for 5 minutes. The dough should be smooth and elastic.

4. Remove dough from machine and knead by hand for 2 to 3 minutes.

5. Place dough in a lightly oiled bowl and cover with clear plastic wrap or a clean towel. Set bowl in a warm place and allow dough to rise until doubled in size, about 25 to 35 minutes.

–This light pizza-style bread tastes best when hot from the oven. Bake just before serving.
–The House Bread will also yield two deep-dish pizza crusts.

Tasty Ways to Enjoy Rolls Tomorrow!
–Slice bread in half, top with tomato sauce and mozzarella cheese, sprinkle with Parmesan cheese and broil.
–Slice bread rolls in finger-size pieces, bake at 350 degrees until golden brown. Mix softened cream cheese and dry onion soup base to use as a dip for baked bread fingers.

*C*huck Muer was a rare blend of business genius and eloquence. ... He was the embodiment of charisma and style. ... He had an unbelievable knack for stepping into a conflict and coming up with a new insight and direction that made the protagonists forget their disagreement and work together with enthusiasm. ... He lived his motto, "If work isn't fun, it isn't worth doing." For instance ... he involved the staffs from all of his Detroit area restaurants in trying to break the Guinness Book of Records mark for the most kites flown on a single line. Kooky? It was fun, and all the media in town showed up on top of Cobo Hall to witness it–and publicize it.

–Bob Moreillon
Robert E. Moreillon Inc.
Livonia, Michigan

6. Mix kosher salt and poppy seeds. Set aside.

7. When the dough has risen, separate it into 4 equal pieces.

8. Sprinkle your work surface with the salt-seed mixture.

9. Form each dough piece into a long loaf and roll through the salt-seed mixture to lightly coat each piece.

10. Place loaves on a baking sheet lined with parchment paper. With kitchen scissors, cut loaves into 5 sections, leaving the sections still attached.

11. Brush loaves completely with Chef Larry's Blessing.

12. Let the loaves rise for 30 minutes before baking. (At this point, they may be refrigerated for up to 8 hours before baking.)

13. Bake at 450 degrees for 10 minutes. Then lower oven temperature to 400 degrees and continue baking another 10 minutes or until golden brown. Serve immediately.

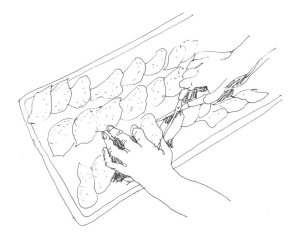

CAESAR SALAD
Recipe by Chef Larry

Yield: 6 servings

2 tablespoons Dijon mustard
Juice of one fresh lemon (1 tablespoon plus 1 teaspoon)
3 medium garlic cloves, peeled
2 large egg yolks
8 anchovies
1 teaspoon Worcestershire sauce
3/4 cup olive oil
1 head romaine lettuce
2 tablespoons Parmesan cheese, freshly grated
1 cup Croutons (see page 20)
6 anchovies for garnish

1. In a blender emulsify mustard, lemon juice, garlic, egg yolks, anchovies and Worcestershire sauce for 1 minute. Be sure to use fresh garlic instead of a prepared garlic product.

2. With the blender on the slowest speed, add olive oil and mix until dressing is well blended and thickened. When finished, it can be covered and refrigerated for up to one week.

3. Wash and dry the romaine. Tear large leaves into 2 pieces.

4. Spread 1/2 cup of dressing on the sides of a wooden salad bowl. Add the romaine leaves, tossing to coat them with the dressing on the side of the bowl. The dressing is very thick and this procedure ensures that all the leaves are well coated.

5. Sprinkle with Parmesan cheese and toss with remaining dressing.

My best memory of Chuck concerned cigars. ... In the early 1970s Chuck helped form a cigar club in Detroit that, I understand, still exists. I was one of the charter members. ... In late 1975, Chuck asked me and a couple other club members if we would be interested in visiting the cigar factories in Tampa and maybe taking a side trip to see the cigar fields in Cuba. Of course, travel to Cuba was prohibited. ... He also said he was trying to set up a meeting with Castro, too. Sure, Chuck, we said skeptically. Look, he said, one of these days the United States would resume trade with Cuba and when that happens those magnificent Cuban cigars would be legal again in this country. And, he said, someone will be needed to import them. Why not C. A. Muer and a couple of his friends? ...

Well, although he tried for a couple years, he never could set up that meeting in Cuba. ... But every time I hear someone talk about a Cuban cigar, I think of Chuck. He might have made me a millionaire.

At least, after dinner at Charley's Crab I would be smoking better cigars. God bless.

–Louis F. Prato
Alexandria, Virginia

To Serve:
Divide salad evenly among 6 plates. Top with Croutons and one fillet of anchovy.

For grilling seafood, poultry or meat use Caesar Salad dressing for a delicious marinade. Also try it brushed on thick slices of Italian bread. Grill the slices and serve with the Caesar Salad.

RICE PILAF
Recipe by Chef Larry

Yield: 6 to 8 servings

2 tablespoons butter for sautéing
1/4 cup onion, finely diced
1 1/2 cups long grain white rice, parboiled
1 1/2 cups chicken broth, fresh or canned
1 1/2 cups beef broth, fresh or canned
1/4 teaspoon salt
2 tablespoons cold butter

1. In a saucepan, melt butter and sauté onions until translucent, 3 to 4 minutes.

2. Add rice, toss well to coat with the butter and onions.

3. Add chicken broth, beef broth and salt.

4. Bring to a boil, then cover and simmer on lowest flame for 12 to 14 minutes or until all broth is absorbed and rice is tender.

5. Immediately put rice into serving bowl and toss with cold butter to coat the rice and prevent sticking. Cold butter halts the cooking process as it coats each grain.

Variations: To the above recipe add 1 cup cooked black beans or 1 cup cooked red beans, or 1/2 cup cooked cracked wheat.
For additional vegetables, try sautéed mushrooms, shredded bok choy, yellow squash, or sautéed colored peppers.

*E*quipped with an infectious grin, bow tie and fat cigar, Chuck Muer soon became Michigan's most innovative restaurateur. ... All of his nineteen eateries ... were different in ambience but fun with value for price. ... Chuck and Betty may be gone physically, but their legacy remains with us, not only for the Muer-inspired innovative designs and food but also for all that they contributed to Michigan in public service.

–Len Barnes
Editor in Chief
Michigan Living

VARIATIONS
To the above recipe add 1 cup cooked black beans, or 1 cup cooked red beans, or 1/2 cup cooked cracked wheat.

For additional vegetables, try sautéed mushrooms, shredded bok choy, yellow squash, or sautéed colored peppers.

This recipe can also be used for stuffing scrod, shrimp, haddock, hake or pollack.

Whatever success I have achieved in the restaurant business is a direct reflection of the guidance, wisdom, and training I received from Chuck Muer. I was blessed to have joined the C. A. Muer Corporation when there was only a handful of restaurants, which enabled me to work hand in hand with Chuck. I miss him dearly.

—John E. Sisson
Leelanau Country Inn
Maple City, Michigan

STUFFED FLOUNDER
Recipe by Chef Larry

Yield: 8 servings

4 pounds flounder (16 small fillets)
Salt to taste
1 recipe Crabmeat Stuffing (see page 29)
1/2 pound crabmeat, preferably Maryland backfin lump
Melted butter
Paprika

1. Make a 2-inch cut through the center of each of 8 fillets Season lightly with salt.

2. Place 1/4 cup of Crabmeat Stuffing in the center of the cut fillets. Set an uncut fillet on top, and roll the pieces together, stopping with the sliced fillet on top.

3. Place stuffed fillets on a baking sheet lined with parchment paper, and evenly distribute the crabmeat into the center of each.

4. Brush fillets with melted butter. Lightly dust with paprika and season with salt.

5. Cover and refrigerate until ready to bake.

6. Preheat oven to 350 degrees. Bake fish for 12 to 15 minutes or until fish flakes with a fork.

To Serve:
Divide cooked, stuffed fillets onto 4 plates. Serve with Rice Pilaf *(See page 26)*.

CHARLEY'S BUCKET

Charley's Crab's signature entree was designed by Chef Larry to be a complete meal – appetizer and main course – and to be an entertaining experience that breaks down inhibitions.

Yield: 2 servings

1 1/2 cups water
1 teaspoon salt
2 ears of fresh corn; leave in husk, trim silk and outer leaves
Two 1 1/4-pound live Maine lobsters
1/2 Dungeness crab, or 1/2-pound king crab legs (thaw if kept frozen)
4 redskin potatoes, precooked
10 mussels, cleaned (see page 17)
10 steamer clams, cleaned (see page 16)
1/2 cup Clarified Butter (see page 12)

1. In a large kettle with a tight-fitting lid, place water and salt. Bring to a boil.

2. Place corn into water, followed by lobsters and crab. Set potatoes alongside the seafood. Cover tightly.

3. Return water to a boil. Cook for 7 minutes. The lobster is fully cooked when the shell is completely red. If dark areas are present, continue to cook.

4. Remove lid and add the mussels and steamers. Cover and steam for 5 additional minutes.

5. Remove lid from kettle and if the mussel and clam shells have opened, the Bucket is done. If shells have not opened, cover and continue steaming until they do.

6. Serve with Clarified Butter for dipping shellfish and crustaceans.

My first recollection of the Muers was the first time we had a fund-raiser at the Retreat House in St. Clair, Michigan. Someone suggested that I should go to Chuck Muer and ask him for a donation toward the golf outing. The thing that I remember most about Chuck was his unassuming manner in meeting me. Here was a businessman with many responsibilities talking to me about what would be best for the Youth Retreat House. ... Probably the charism that Chuck and his wife leave for us is their constant care and awareness of all walks of life. To them, anyone they met was important, no matter who you were.

–Brother Michael Graf,
Capuchin
Past Director, St. Clair
Retreat House

ROUX

A roux is the most common thickener for soups and sauces. It is made by combining and cooking together equal amounts of flour and fats. A roux not only thickens, but also enhances the flavor of the finished product.

When I think of Chuck Muer ... I think of dancing eyes, a warm smile, an insatiable zest for living. When Chuck walked into a room, you felt his presence. I likened his presence to the strings of a harp which fill a room with music that everyone enjoys. I shall always treasure the many hours I spent with Chuck in all the community work we shared together.

–Diane J. Edgecomb
President, Central Business
District Association
Detroit

CRABMEAT STUFFING
Recipe by Chef Larry

Yield:

1 1/2 tablespoons Clarified Butter (see page 12) for cream sauce
1 1/2 tablespoons flour
1 1/2 cups milk
1/4 cup Clarified Butter
1/2 cup onions, finely chopped
1 pound backfin lump crabmeat, shells removed
3/4 cup dried bread crumbs

1. First make a cream sauce: In a small saucepan, cook together at a low heat 1 1/2 tablespoons of Clarified Butter and the flour. Do not brown. Set aside.

2. Heat the milk and slowly add to the butter-flour mixture to form a roux *(see side note).* Cook on low heat until thickened, 3 to 5 minutes, to finish your cream sauce.

3. Cool cream sauce to room temperature before using in the Crabmeat Stuffing.

4. In a saucepan, heat 1/4 cup Clarified Butter and sauté onions until translucent. Place onions and butter into a mixing bowl and set aside.

5. While the onions are cooling, remove the shells from the crabmeat. Toss crabmeat gently with the bread crumbs.

6. After the onions and butter have cooled, fold them into the cream sauce.

7. Then fold the cream sauce mixture into crabmeat and bread crumbs, mixing gently with a rubber spatula. Be careful not to break up crabmeat.

8. Refrigerate until ready to serve. Stuffing will keep for up to 5 days. This recipe can be used for stuffing shrimp, sole or scrod.

Signature Recipes

LOBSTER LARRY with Crabmeat Stuffing
Recipe by Chef Larry

Chef Larry created this signature dish of lobster stuffed with crabmeat and mushrooms for the Hotel Pontchartrain's rooftop supper club, Cabaret La Boheme.

Yield: 4 servings

Four 1 1/4-pound live Maine lobsters
1 cup button mushrooms, sliced 1/4-inch thick
1 recipe of Crabmeat Stuffing (see page 29)
4 tablespoons Clarified Butter (see page 12)
1/2 teaspoon paprika

1. Steam lobsters in a large pot for 6 minutes, or until back and claws have turned red. Cool.

2. In a mixing bowl, fold sliced mushrooms into Crabmeat Stuffing. Set aside.

3. Place each lobster on its back and split in half lengthwise from head to tail with a large knife. Remove stomach and intestines. Be careful to leave tail meat sections and greenish-brown tomalley intact.

4. Crack lobster claws. A wooden mallet or large kitchen spoon works well for this.

5. Divide stuffing evenly and place in body cavity of each lobster half. Brush stuffing and tail meat with Clarified Butter and sprinkle with paprika.

6. Place on baking sheet. Cover and refrigerate until ready to heat and serve.

In the place of backfin lump crabmeat, you can also use Jonah crab leg meat, king crabmeat, or cooked flaked salmon.

*I*t's hard to imagine two people with a greater zest for life than Betty and Chuck. Sue remembers her trip down the mountain from Aspen to Denver in a blinding snowstorm in convulsions of laughter at Betty's wonderful stories. I remember running the bulls in Pomplona, Spain, with Chuck in 1991. He stepped into the street sight unseen. Chuck was a real man's man.

–Dick Measelle
Managing Partner,
Arthur Andersen & Co.
New York City

*B*eing a food writer, I always felt close to Chuck because he was so accessible. So smart. So creative. And so friendly. One of the most fun stories we ever did together was showing people how to eat a lobster when you're all dressed up. Wearing a tuxedo, he delicately dismantled one and picked out every last morsel without getting it all over him. He made it look so easy. He was a born showman. ... Chuck Muer was a revolutionary in the restaurant industry for the dynamic way he handled business and the sensitive way he treated people. Everybody in the industry copied Chuck. Not enough gave him credit.

–Sandra Silfven
Staff Writer, Copy Editor
The Detroit News

To Serve:
1. Preheat oven to 350 degrees.

2. Bake lobsters for 15 to 20 minutes or until stuffing is hot, about 160 degrees.

Although this recipe specifies 1 1/4-pound lobsters, it will work with lobsters of any size. It depends on how much you want to eat and how much fun you want to have. A split and stuffed 4- or 5-pound lobster dominating the middle of the table makes a festive conversation piece.

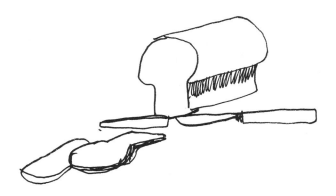

KEY LIME PIE
Recipe by Chef Rick Davis

Yield: one 10-inch pie

1 1/2 cups graham cracker crumbs
3 tablespoons sugar
3 tablespoons unsalted butter, melted
10 egg yolks
Two 14-ounce cans sweetened condensed milk
1 1/4 cups Key lime juice
1 lime, cut into wedges for garnish

1. Mix crumbs, sugar and melted butter together and press evenly on sides and bottom of a 10-inch pie pan.

2. Bake crust 10 minutes in a 325 degree oven. Set aside while making the filling.

3. In a large bowl, whisk together egg yolks and sweetened condensed milk until smooth.

4. Add the Key lime juice. It is important to add the lime juice last because the acid of the juice will curdle the egg yolks if added sooner.

5. Pour lime mixture into baked pie shell and bake 15 to 20 minutes in a 325 degree oven.

6. Cool at room temperature. Then refrigerate overnight, or for at least 5 hours.

To Serve:
1. Cut cold pie and set on individual dishes.

2. Garnish with fresh lime wedges. Squeeze the wedge over the pie for a more intense citrus flavor.

Key limes are very different from the common green Persian lime in taste and color. Key limes look like small lemons, are yellow, very acidic and almost bitter. Florida Key lime juice is available at most specialty food stores. The source for our restaurants, Key West Lime Juice in Miami, can give you the name and location of a distributor in your area. Call (305) 233-5987.

Soups

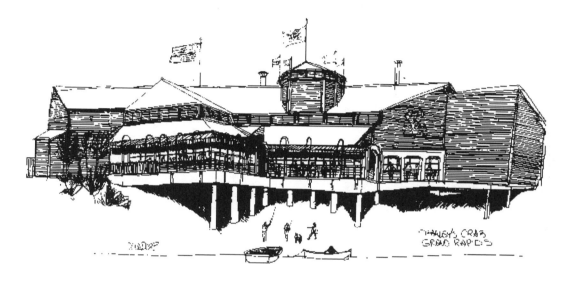

Charley's Crab, Grand Rapids, Michigan . . . a serene view of the Grand
River from the glass-walled, multi-level dining room, just down the street
from the Gerald Ford Presidential Library

ROASTED GARLIC SOUP
HAROLD'S MATZO BALL SOUP
CORN & HAM CHOWDER
BIG FISH CHOWDER
MANHATTAN CLAM CHOWDER
VICHYSOISSE

I grew up in old Grosse Pointe Park. ... Chuck and Betty and I were good friends through all those years growing up and well into our adulthood. We shared in some sorrows and difficulties, but mainly when I think of Chuck and Betty, I think of the good times–good times and good places. And always the laughter. ... Generative, generous, always of service, sharing their wealth, knowledge and wisdom in all their attempts to help others grow and flourish. I miss my friends and regret that the story couldn't have ended differently. If only Neptune, king of the seas, had intervened and disarmed that violent storm of the century.

–Alex Wortman
Alex Wortman &
Associates
Ann Arbor, Michigan

ROASTED GARLIC SOUP
Recipe by Chef Jim Blake

While on a trip in Austria, our general managers were served this hearty soup. We were so impressed with this dish, when we got back to the states, Chef Jim Blake modified it for our restaurants. Chuck Muer would have saluted this dish because of its simple preparation and wonderful flavor.

Yield: 8 servings

1 whole bulb of garlic, peeled
7 cups chicken broth
1 cup heavy cream
1 leek, 2-inch large dice
1/2 cup onion, 2-inch large dice
1/3 cup scallion, large chop
Salt & pepper to taste
1 cup Croutons (see page 20)

1. Place the garlic bulbs, leeks, onions and scallions in a small roasting pan. Add 2 cups of the chicken broth and place in a preheated 350 degree oven. Roast the mixture for 1 hour, stirring occasionally until the garlic is mushy.

2. Remove from oven add 1 cup chicken broth and purée the mixture. Strain the mixture through a china cap and place in a saucepan.

3. Add the rest of the chicken broth (4 cups) and the heavy creme to the sauce pan.

4. Bring to a boil and simmer on medium low heat for 45 minutes.

5. Adjust seasoning.

To Serve:
1. Place in 8 bowls and garnish with the croutons.

HAROLD'S MATZO BALL SOUP
Vision of the late Harold Kaplan

This soup is named after Harold Kaplan. Harold was not only a mentor to Chuck Muer, but also is the "Harold"of Chuck and Harold's in Palm Beach, Florida. Harold believed this soup could cure any illness. As Harold would say, "A cup a day keeps the doctors away."

Yield: 6 to 8 servings

4 eggs
1 teaspoon kosher salt
3 tablespoons olive oil
1 teaspoons baking powder
1 cup matzo meal
2 quarts chicken broth, canned, or homemade
1 cup chicken meat, cooked and diced
4 teaspoons scallion, sliced for garnish

To Make Matzo Balls:

1. In a mixing bowl beat the eggs, salt and olive oil together. Whisk together well.

2. In a separate bowl mix together the baking powder and matzo meal.

3. Add the matzo meal to the egg mixture. Mix well. Refrigerate for 30 minutes.

4. Remove matzo mix from refrigerator, portion 2 table spoons and mold into 1 1/2-inch balls. Portion all into balls.

*A*fter closing the Red Garter Saloon in downtown Detroit, I went into the night club tour business with Dennis Horwatt. We figured the fun way of transporting people to night spots around the downtown area would be by London double-decker bus. And just our luck, Chuck Muer had one for sale. After about a year, Detroit Tonight Tours needed another double-decker to handle the growing business. After finding one, we decided to have a local priest marry the buses.

The wedding ceremony, after a long police-escorted parade down Woodward Avenue, took place in the

middle of the Kern block. The buses were appropriately decorated in a veil and top hat, and Chuck Muer, the best man, graciously gave the bride away (his former bus was "female"). Chuck also christened the happy couple by pouring a vintage bottle of champagne over their radiator caps. Who else but Chuck Muer would relish in participating in the craziest wedding ceremony I've ever witnessed? Thank you, Chuck, for the memories.

–Doug Jacobs
Red Garter Band
Waterford, Michigan

To Serve:

1. Grill or poach chicken. Dice or chop into medium-size cubes.

2. Bring the chicken broth to a boil. Add the matzo balls. Turn down heat and simmer for 30 minutes.

3. Place 10 ounces of the hot chicken broth into 4 soup bowls. Add 4 tablespoons of chicken meat in each bowl with 2 matzo balls.

4. Garnish each bowl with 1 teaspoon of the sliced scallions.

CORN & HAM CHOWDER
Recipe by Chef Jim Blake

Yield: 4 to 6 servings

1/2 stick butter
1/2 cup flour
1/2 gallon water
4 tablespoons smokey ham base—OR—use the 1/2 gallon
    water cooked with a ham bone
2 tablespoons corn oil or bacon fat
1 cup onion, diced
1/2 green pepper, diced
1/4 red pepper, diced
1 teaspoon garlic, minced
3 1/4 tablespoons celery, chopped
1 green onion, chopped
1 cup corn, fresh off the cob
1 cup ham, diced
1/2 cup tasso pork (Cajun-style pork available at finer meat
    markets)
3 tablespoons tomato purée
1 1/4 cups heavy cream
Salt & pepper to taste

1. Add the ham base to the 1/2 gallon of water, mix well, set aside.

2. Melt butter in saucepan, whisk in flour and cook 10 minutes on very low heat, stirring occasionally with a wooden spoon.

3. Slowly add ham stock while whisking vigorously, this will help avoid lumps. Simmer on low heat.

Meanwhile:
4. Add oil or bacon fat to a sauté pan, add onions, celery, peppers, garlic, ham, tasso pork and corn.

5. Sauté 10 to 12 minutes.

Chuck's great remark, "Kites aren't for kids," is aptly demonstrated by a kite "tale." ... Can you imagine the looks on the faces of most of the SORC, Miami to Nassau race crews at the Nassau Yacht Haven as they watched a champagne bottle (tied unseen by Chuck to a 4,400-foot flying kite) snake and surf its way through the masts and rigging of the docked fleet, throwing a magnificent wake as it planed its course across the harbor until it crashed on the rocky shore of Paradise Island? Chuck had launched a large colorful eaglelike kite—tethered by eleven, four-hundred-foot spools of string tied together—off the stern of the sloop Mars as it headed south en route to Miami. Our memories of Chuck and Betty soar higher than his kites.

–Stew and Dot McKeough
McKeough Sons, Ltd.
Chatham, Ontario

 Soups

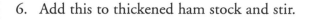

6. Add this to thickened ham stock and stir.

7. Add tomato purée and stir.

8. Slowly add cream and stir.

9. Simmer 45 minutes.

10. Salt & pepper to taste.

*M*y memories of Chuck go back to the 1960s when he took over the catering of the Hotel Pontchartrain. He was a master greeter and a consummate maitre d', which our Lincoln-Mercury dealers enjoyed at the new hotel. I feel privileged that he touched my life. Our association was special, as are the memories of him. God bless the Muers.

–Bernard R. Brown Jr.
White Lake, Michigan

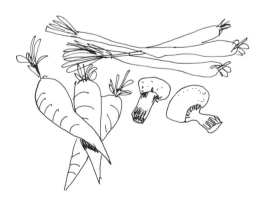

BIG FISH CHOWDER
Recipe by Chef Chuck "Rocky" Rachwitz

This soup was created for the Big Fish restaurant in Dearborn, Michigan. It is a playoff on the traditional New England Clam Chowder and is less thick in consistency than the New England. Big Fish Chowder receives its smoky flavor not from bacon but from smoked finnan haddie.

Yield: 6 servings

2 quarts water
4 tablespoons clam base
      —OR—
Substitute 2 quarts clam juice for the above
2 1/2 cups cooked red skin potatoes (leave skins on), diced
Three 6 1/2-ounce cans chopped clams
1 1/2 tablespoons olive oil
2 1/2 tablespoons tasso pork (Cajun Style pork available at finer meat markets)
1 cup onions, diced
3/4 cup celery, diced
1/2 teaspoon basil, dried
1/2 teaspoon oregano, dried
1/4 cup red bell pepper, diced
1/4 cup green bell pepper, diced
1/2 stick butter
1/2 cup flour
1 cup finnan haddie (smoked haddock)
1/2 cup raw salmon, diced
1/2 cup raw white fish (halibut, walleye or grouper), diced
2/3 cup whipping cream
1 1/2 tablespoons chopped parsley
4 teaspoons fresh tomatoes, diced; to be used for garnish in each bowl, 1 teaspoon per serving

1. Melt butter in a large saucepan, whisk in flour and cook 10 minutes on very low heat, stirring occasionally with a wooden spoon.

I loved Chuck. He was much more than a fine and highly respected restaurateur. He was a wonderful person who endeared himself into the hearts of whoever met him. He and I went back to the opening of the restaurants at Hotel Pontchartrain, and through the years I was always proud to call him a friend.

–Danny Raskin
The Jewish News
Southfield, Michigan

If soup is too thick ... thin with cream or Half & Half or milk.

There are two things about Chuck Muer that I will always remember. First, his unqualified love for the restaurant business itself, whether he was working on a food recipe, designing a new restaurant or teaching a manager how to take care of our guests. ... Second, his love for the people who make up our business. From the managers to the waitstaff, the cooks to the bartenders, and most of all our guests, Chuck truly celebrated the people he came into contact with. Once, as he and I were discussing whether or not to spend considerable money to remodel a restaurant, Chuck said, "We will always invest in people, not buildings, and this manager deserves to see his vision of this restaurant come true." That, in a nutshell, was Chuck Muer..

–Roger Zingle
Vice President
C. A. Muer Corporation
Pittsburgh

2. Slowly add clam juice to butter and flour mixture while whisking vigorously (be sure to use a wire whip); this will help avoid lumps.

3. Simmer on low heat.

While stock is simmering:

4. Add oil and heat in a sauté pan, add tasso pork, celery, onions, basil, and oregano.

5. Sauté 7 to 10 minutes until vegetables are soft and translucent.

6. Add red and green peppers and sauté another 2 to 3 minutes.

7. Add vegetable/tasso mixture to stock, stir.

8. Simmer on low heat for 10 minutes.

9. Add finnan haddie, salmon and white fish. Simmer another 10 minutes.

10. Slowly add whipping cream, canned clams, cooked red skins and parsley. Simmer on medium heat for 30 minutes and serve. Or cool down and refrigerate and reheat when needed.

11. Garnish each bowl with 1 teaspoon chopped red ripe tomatoes. In winter use roma plum tomatoes because they are the only tomato that will ripen to a bright red and taste like a summer tomato.

Soups

MANHATTAN CLAM CHOWDER
Recipe by Chef Chuck "Rocky" Rachwitz

Yield: 8 to 10 servings

3/4 gallon warm water
2 tablespoons butter
1 cup onion, diced
1/2 cup celery, diced
1/2 cup carrots, diced
2 cups potatoes, diced
3 cups fresh tomatoes, peeled, diced
1/2 cup tomato puree
2 tablespoons parsley, chopped fine
3 cups chopped clams with juice
1 teaspoon basil
1 teaspoon oregano
1/2 teaspoon thyme
2 tablespoons kosher salt

1. In a medium saucepan bring water to a boil and add the diced potatoes. Cook for 15 minutes or until soft. DO NOT overcook. Remove from pan and cool completely under cold water. Set aside.

2. In a large stock (soup) pot melt the butter. Add the onion, celery, basil, parsley, oregano, thyme, and cook until translucent. Add the carrots and sauté for 3 minutes.

3. Add the warm water, tomatoes, tomato purée, clams, parsley, potatoes, and kosher salt to the stock pot. Bring to a boil, reduce heat, cover and simmer for 1 hour.

I am a jazz promoter. ... When Chuck wanted to do jazz poolside [at the Hotel Pontchartrain], he called me and I helped him book the big bands into the P-JAZZ series. ... We became fast friends. I loved him tenderly. One time, Stan Kenton's band was playing. The baritone [sax] player was a doll and a good-looking young woman kept buying him drinks. ... As the band finished ... the baritone player stayed behind talking to the woman. Suddenly, her boyfriend grabbed the sax man and threatened to bust his lip and leave him unable to play again. ... He and the boyfriend began circling each other. ... I searched the crowd for help and saw Chuck. ... He ran between them, trying to separate them. They both towered over Chuck. Finally, he came back to me. ... We went to a nearby table. "Nothing like a ringside seat, Midge," he said. ... Chuck knew when to get involved. That's why he was so successful.

—Midge Ellis
Livonia, Michigan

I've kept [this letter from Chuck Muer to the board of directors of the Detroit Athletic Club] as an example of Chuck's friendship and good humor:

"Gentlemen,

"RE: Karl Bennett Membership

"Karl Bennett has been a personal friend and business associate for over twenty years. I have the highest regard for Karl and enthusiastically endorse his membership.

"P.S. In retrospect though, does the DAC need another attorney? Does our country? Does anybody?"

–Karl R. Bennett Jr.
Attorney at Law
Detroit

VICHYSOISSE
Recipe by Chef Chuck "Rocky" Rachwitz

Vichysoisse is a classic French "chilled" soup. We offered this soup on the first menu in the La Mediterranee at the Hotel Pontchartrain in the mid 1960s. Vichysoisse was one of Betty Muer's favorite soups.

Yield: 6 servings

1 pound potatoes
48 ounces chicken stock or canned chicken broth
1/4 teaspoon Worcestershire sauce
1/2 cup onions, medium diced
2 leeks (whites only)
2 tablespoons butter
1 bay leaf
Pinch of thyme, dried
1 1/3 cups heavy cream
2 tablespoons sliced chives
1/2 cup sour cream
Salt & white pepper to taste

1. In a soup pot, melt the butter. Sauté leeks and onions until translucent. Add bay leaf and thyme and cook 30 seconds.

2. Add chicken stock and potatoes, bring to a boil and simmer 30 minutes until potatoes are soft.

3. Remove from heat and wait until soup is warm. When warm, purée in blender, being careful lid is on tight, or in a food processor.

4. Add heavy cream, salt and pepper, and chill.

5. Serve with a dollop of sour cream and the chives.

Soups

Appetizers & LightEntrées

CHARLEY'S CRAB
TROY

Charley's Crab, Troy, Michigan . . . *housing the great room of an auto baron's Grosse Pointe mansion, with music played by masters of ragtime and jazz piano*

SMOKED SALMON QUESADILLA
OYSTERS WITH CHAMPAGNE SAUCE
BARBECUE SHRIMP
SALMON TARTARE
SMOKED WHITEFISH PATÉ
SEARED YELLOWFIN TUNA SASHIMI
CRABMEAT BALLS
CLAMS PETER
SHERRY BUTTERED CAPE SCALLOPS
SALSA MEXICANA

SMOKED SALMON QUESADILLA
Recipe by Chef Jim Blake

Yield: 4 servings

Two 10-inch flour tortillas (at room temperature for flexibility)
6 tablespoons Boursin cheese (available at most grocery stores)
1/4 cup ripe Plum (Roma) tomatoes, medium diced
2 teaspoons fresh dill, chopped
1 teaspoon capers, drained
4 ounces smoked salmon
1 tablespoon olive oil
1 cup sour cream
3 tablespoons fresh dill
8 tablespoons Salsa Mexicana (see page 64)

1. Place the sour cream and 3 tablespoons fresh dill into a blender and mix until very green and smooth. Set aside.

2. Take each tortilla and spread equal amounts of the Boursin cheese on only 1/2 of each tortilla.

3. Top the cheese with 1 tablespoon diced tomatoes, 1/2 teaspoon dill and 1/2 teaspoon capers. Add 1 ounce smoked salmon to each, then fold in half.

4. Place the olive oil into a heated 12-inch sauté pan. Add the tortilla and sauté on medium heat until golden brown. Turn over and brown the other side.

To Serve:
1. Remove tortilla from sauté pan and place on a large round platter. Cut each quesadilla into 4 triangles. Drizzle the sour cream/dill sauce on top to garnish, sprinkle with two teaspoons fresh chopped dill.

2. Place Salsa Mexicana on the side.

Appetizers & Light Entrées ———— 51

OYSTERS WITH CHAMPAGNE SAUCE
Recipe by Chef Chuck "Rocky" Rachwitz

This appetizer was created for the opening of Big Fish in Dearborn, Michigan. Great to eat and easy to prepare, this dish inspires awe in guests because of it's beautiful presentation.

Yield: 4 appetizer servings

3 cups leeks, white part and 1 inch of green, 1/8" x 2" julienne cut
1 tablespoon fennel seed
1/4 cup butter
1/2 teaspoon salt
12 bluepoint oysters, shucked, reserve juice (see page 14)
2 tablespoons butter
3 ounces champagne
5 ounces heavy cream

1. Heat a large sauté pan, add the butter, leeks, fennel and salt. Sauté on medium heat until the leeks are limp, about 15 minutes. Be careful not to burn the leeks.

2. Shuck the oysters *(see page 14)*, save the juice. Remove oysters from the shell and set aside. Save the bottom, deeper shells.

3. After the leeks have cooled, place 2 tablespoons of the leek mixture in each of the saved shells (12 shells). Refrigerate until needed.

4. Heat a small sauté pan, add 2 tablespoons of butter, add the shucked oysters and the saved juice. Heat the oysters just until they start to wrinkle, remove oysters.

5. Place the poached oysters (1 per oyster shell) on top of the leek mixture. Place oyster shells into a preheated 350 degree oven to warm for 5 minutes.

Chuck Muer was a good friend of the Historical Society of Michigan and of history in general. He had a keen appreciation of the importance of history in our lives and in our understanding of contemporary society. Testimony to that belief can be seen in his attention to detail in the restoration and operation of his Gandy Dancer restaurant in the nineteenth century train depot in Ann Arbor. ... Seeking notable events and occasions to honor the twentieth anniversary of the Gandy Dancer in 1991, Chuck invited the board of trustees of the Historical Society of Michigan to hold one of its quarterly meetings at the restaurant. ... Additionally ... he knew that the state governmental agency for history, the Michigan Historical Commission, also played a key role in promoting statewide knowledge of Michigan's fascinating history.

His suggestion was a simple one: if he was going to host a meeting of the trustees of the Historical Society of Michigan, why not simultaneously host a meeting of the Michigan Historical Commissioners? ... What is notable about that 1991 luncheon is that it was the first joint meeting ... in thirty years! The causes for this decades-long division are too complicated to discuss here. What is important is that Chuck Muer's reputation and position in Michigan successfully overcame decades of separation between these two panels. Dining and meeting in the historic ambiance of the Gandy Dancer worked wonders that day, a day that concluded with the commitment to meet annually. And so it has been. ... That moment was a special one and will remain firmly in my recollections of a very special person, Chuck Muer.

–Thomas L. Jones
Executive Director
Historical Society of
Michigan
Ann Arbor, Michigan

6. Add the champagne to the sauté pan with the oyster juice and reduce by half.

7. Add the heavy cream and reduce until slightly thickened.

To Serve:
1. Place the hot oyster shells on 4 plates. Pour the champagne sauce equally over each plate. Serve immediately.

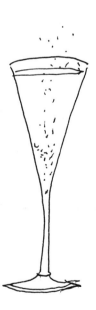

 Appetizers & Light Entrées ———— *53*

BARBECUE SHRIMP
Recipe by Chef Chuck "Rocky" Rachwitz

Yield: 8 servings

24 large shrimp, peeled and deveined
12 slices bacon, half cooked, cut in half lengthwise.

Barbecue Sauce:
1 1/2 cups orange juice concentrate
6 tablespoons soy sauce
1 cup ketchup
3/4 cup molasses
4 teaspoons Worcestershire sauce
2 teaspoons Tabasco
1 1/2 cups chili sauce
2 tablespoons Dijon mustard
2 cloves garlic, chopped fine
2 tablespoons fresh lemon juice
1/2 cup chicken broth
2 teaspoons salt

1. Peel and devein the shrimp, leaving the tail on.

2. Cook the bacon halfway in a skillet, chill, cut in half lengthwise.

3. Wrap the shrimp in bacon holding together with a tooth pick.

4. In a large bowl mix together all the ingredients for the BBQ sauce.

5. Place the bacon wrapped shrimp on the sheet tray.

6. Ladle the BBQ sauce generously over each shrimp, leaving the tails unsauced.

Chicken can be substituted for the shrimp.

*C*huck set new standards for the restaurant industry. He was creative, fun and sometimes wild, but most of all he produced success with quality. His unique style and flair brought new recipes and fresh seafood to the tables of America that had never seen this before. But Chuck's success story was not for himself. He made others successful and directly assisted the careers of many restaurateurs who were his former employees. We were the closest of friends, enjoying our work and play together. I won't have such a friendly competitor like this again and neither will the industry. His contributions are without peer and this journal of food, wine, friends and history will be long lasting.

—Joseph W. Muer Jr.
Joe Muer Sea Food
Detroit

Much to my great disappointment, I never really had the opportunity to know Chuck Muer. ... On the three occasions that our paths crossed, the thing I can truly say without reservation is that he was one of those rare people who just glowed. His manner and magnetism drew you to him from all four corners of the room, no matter the distance.

–Steven Dicker
General Manager
Muer's Seafood
Boca Raton, Florida

7. Place the shrimp under a low heat broiler, cook for 6 minutes. Turn shrimp and cook for another 6 minutes.

To Serve:
Place the shrimp on a large decorative platter, with napkins on the side.

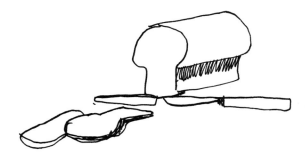

SALMON TARTARE
Recipe by Chef Peter Ashcraft

Yield : 8 serving

2 pounds salmon, must be fresh, chopped fine
1 egg yolk, room temperature
1 tablespoon red wine vinegar
1/2 cup extra virgin olive oil
1/2 teaspoon Dijon mustard
1/4 tablespoon sherry vinegar
2 tablespoons parsley, chopped
2 tablespoons capers, chopped
2 tablespoons pickle (dill or cornichon), chopped
2 tablespoons shallots, chopped
Salt & pepper to taste
1 medium avocado

1. Place the room temperature egg yolk in a bowl and slowly whisk in the red wine vinegar.

2. Very slowly whisk in the olive oil, keep adding olive oil slowly to yolk mixture. The sauce should have a consistency of mayonnaisse. (Whip vigorously and add a little more olive oil if needed to thin.)

3. Add all of the remaining ingredients to the mayonnaise mixture. Sauce may be made ahead of time and chilled at this point for later.

4. Take salmon and remove any bones and skin. Chop the salmon very fine. Cover with saran and chill.

To Serve:
1. In a bowl mix the salmon with the sauce mixture. Serve on toast points with slice of avocado, or in a decorative bowl with toast points on the side.

Salmon must be of the freshest quality and used on the same day purchased. Tuna and beef tenderloin can also be substituted for the salmon.

Shortly after I moved to D. C., I was talking with Donna Bauer. I told her the things I thought this restaurant was capable of and that I felt it had been abused by previous management. She suggested that I write these thoughts in a letter to Chuck. Well, I did. ... The phone rang one morning and it was Chuck. He was thrilled with the letter and said he would be passing through D. C. soon and would stop and have a chat with Gene and me. It was late one evening and Chuck and Betty had been driving from Florida to see the new baby. Gene and I greeted them with a big hug, seated them and cooked them a nice meal. We talked for about an hour sharing our thoughts of this restaurant and its potential. ... After Gene had shared his ideas about food and cooking, Chuck said he was so proud that two people who were getting married cared so much about his restaurant. Betty gave me a big hug and said the restaurant looked great. Gene and I never forgot that night, because the last thing Chuck said was, "If you two keep up the good work, this restaurant will be yours someday." That was the nicest thing anyone could have said to us. We were thrilled with the dream of running a Chuck Muer restaurant someday.

–Cheri and Gene Guazzo
Charley's Crab
Washington, D. C.

Paté may be prepped up to a day ahead and baked at service. It is also great chilled.

SMOKED WHITEFISH PATÉ
Recipe by Chef Chuck "Rocky" Rachwitz

This dish was created for our Annual Whitefish Festival, which goes on in our restaurants during the late summer months when whitefish are plentiful in the Great Lakes.

Yield: 10 to 12 servings

1/2 pound smoked whitefish
3/4 pound cream cheese, room temperature
2 tablespoons horesradish
1/2 teaspoon ground black pepper
1 teaspoon Tabasco sauce
2 teaspoons parsley, chopped, for garnish

1. Remove any skin and bones from whitefish.

2. Place the cream cheese and whitefish in a food processor and whip until smooth.

3. Add the horseradish, pepper and Tabasco and purée for 1 minute.

4. Divide the paté into 4 ramekins or place in a casserole dish and bake in a preheated 375 degree oven for 10 minutes.

5. Garnish with chopped parsley.

6. Serve with matzo crackers.

SEARED YELLOWFIN TUNA SASHIMI
Recipe by Chef Jim Blake

Chuck Muer believed that tuna when really fresh, should be eaten like meat. Cooking the tuna medium rare to rare seals in the juices and eats like a juicy filet mignon.

Yield: 4 servings

3/4 pound yellowfin tuna, must be fresh
1 ounce Wasabi powder
1 ounce olive oil
1 ounce soy sauce

Garnish:
1/8 ounce Wasabi powder mixed with water to form a paste
1/4 ounce pickled sushi ginger
4 watercress sprigs (for garnish)

1. Mix together the Wasabi powder, olive oil and soy sauce.

2. Rub both sides of the tuna with the Wasabi powder, olive oil, soy sauce mixture.

3. Cover with plastic wrap and refrigerate tuna, marinate for one (1) hour.

4. Remove from refrigerator and place on preheated hot grill.

5. Cook until only 1/8 inch into tuna is cooked, center MUST be rare/raw.

6. Let cool (refrigerate) for 1 hour.

7. Wrap with cling film and place in freezer for 15 minutes (this will firm the tuna and allow you to cut it).

A Japanese dish of raw fish. The fish, which must always be very fresh, is trimmed and boned.

*B*etty and Chuck, two kind, loving, generous people. You will always be in our hearts and prayers. God bless your family. With love forever.

–Aunt Rose
(Mrs. Edwin F. Sanders)
Grosse Pointe, Michigan

I would like to commemorate Chuck Muer for his significant contribution to the preservation and adaption of historic structures into exciting and viable restaurants. Although today this type of restoration seems commonplace, at the time the Gandy Dancer, Engine House and Grand Concourse were transformed he was one of the pioneers of historic restoration and adaption. These were complex projects and Chuck provided the enthusiasm, vision and leadership to transform these spaces. Because of Chuck's vision, these structures were preserved for future generations to enjoy their history and beauty along with having a unique dining experience.

–Joy Walker
Partner
Roger Sherman Partners
Inc.
Dearborn, Michigan

8. Slice 1/8 inch thick, across the grain
   (1" x 3" x 6").

Plate Setup:
1. Use four 9-inch round plates.

2. Place 3 ounces of sliced tuna in the center of each plate.

3. Garnish each with Wasabi paste (Wasabi powder mixed with water), pickled ginger and watercress sprig.

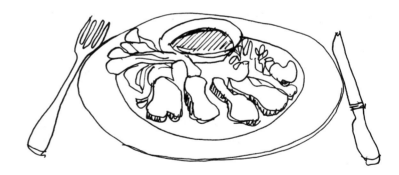

CRABMEAT BALLS
Recipe by Chef Loretto "Larry" Pagliara

Yield: 45 half-ounce balls
10 to 12 servings

2 pounds deluxe crabmeat, preferably canned fresh pasteurized
2 tablespoons bread crumbs
1 teaspoon dry mustard
1 egg, beaten
4 1/4 tablespoons mayonnaise
1 teaspoon chopped fresh parsley
1/2 teaspoon Worcestershire sauce
1/4 teaspoon prepared mustard
Touch of salt and white pepper
2 tablespoons dry mustard
1 cup cracker meal
1 cup milk
1 cup Cajun Remoulade Sauce, for dipping (see page 6)
Parchment paper
Vegetable oil or canola oil

1. Open cans of crabmeat, place in a bowl and remove shells from crabmeat, being careful not to break up crabmeat. Set aside.

2. In a separate bowl combine the egg, mayonnaise, parsley, Worcestershire, prepared mustard, salt, pepper and mix well.

3. Add 1 teaspoon dry mustard to the crabmeat, toss well. Add the bread crumbs, toss well, again being careful NOT to break up the crabmeat.

4. Fold egg mixture into bread crumb-crab mixture.

5. Cover and refrigerate mixture for 1 hour.

Chuck Muer was and still is a great inspiration in my continuing the philosophy and values of guest relations, food presentation, and staff involvement. ... Chuck was such an explosive man in the positive sense. He would be able to motivate me just by talking about the possibilities a person has. ... I have continued for eight years with the C. A. Muer Corporation because of the values it holds and the excellence in all we do.

–Ellen Daly
General Manager
Charley's Crab
Deerfield Beach, FL

In the seventeen years that I knew Chuck, there were many great moments: sailing, skiing, fishing, hunting, playing tennis, squash and gin. He helped me become reasonably good at all of them. His enthusiasm and energy for life and his great passion for the outdoors made him a good teacher. He also had a way about him that could make simple times seem very special: going to London Dairy for a shake, working on a jigsaw puzzle, or learning to eat oysters with lemon and pepper and all the conversation and humor that went with it. Chuck's friendship was a special gift to me that I hold close to my heart. His spirit will be part of me always.

—Sue DiBiase-Nicholl
Grosse Pointe Woods
Michigan

6. Remove mixture from refrigerator, form balls weighing approximately 1/2-ounce each (about 45).

7. Place parchment paper on a sheet tray then place each crabmeat ball on the paper, cover with plastic wrap and refrigerate for 1 more hour or until the balls become firm.

8. Remove tray from refrigerator, sprinkle the crabmeat balls with dry mustard and shake the pan to cover them evenly.

9. Place 1 cup of milk (milk wash) in a bowl. Dip each crabmeat ball individually in milk wash, quickly remove and roll in cracker meal. Replenish milk and cracker meal if needed.

10. Heat vegetable or canola oil in a sauce pan to 350 degrees and fry until crispy.

11. Serve with lemon wedges and Cajun Remoulade Sauce for dipping.

Appetizers & Light Entrées

CLAMS PETER
Recipe by Chef Peter Ashcraft

Yield: 12 servings

36 littleneck clams, fresh, shucked (see page16)
1/2 cup roasted, peeled and chopped hazelnuts
4 cups white wine
1 bay leaf
1/4 teaspoon nutmeg, ground
1/4 teaspoon thyme, dried
1 1/4 pounds of butter
4 ounces peeled chopped garlic
4 ounces peeled chopped shallots
1 tablespoon clam base
1 tablespoon arrowroot
2 tablespoons chopped parsley

1. In a stainless steel pot, reduce the wine with the bay leaf, nutmeg and thyme until almost evaporated, about 1/2 cup remaining. Strain and set aside.

2. In another stainless steel heavy bottom pot, melt 1/2 pound of the butter and sweat the shallots and garlic, stirring and not letting the heat get high enough to brown. About 4 minutes.

3. Add strained wine, clam base and remaining butter, which should be diced up for easier melting. Keep heat low until all butter is melted.

4. Mix the arrowroot with 1 tablespoon water. Add the arrowroot slowly to the garlic butter. Let butter thicken over low heat for 1 minute.

5. Remove from heat, place butter in the refrigerator for 45 minutes to chill.

6. Shuck the clams and top each with 2 table spoons of the clam butter, top with the hazelnuts and chopped parsley and bake at 400 degrees until butter is melted.

One story I would like to share has become the nucleus of my vision and made me a successful proprietor of Charley's Crab. The day after Chuck Muer finished his book signing for The Simply Great Cookbook here in Beachwood, Chuck and Betty invited my wife, Sandra, and I to join them for dinner. At that dinner many stories were shared about work, family, and life. Then Chuck made a comment to me that I have taken to heart. He said he knew I was the "right man" for the restaurant and the community through the feelings he received from the guests, the employees and the general atmosphere of the restaurant. ... Chuck's commitment to me will carry on as I have adopted what he taught me to be a successful proprietor, or as Chuck used to say, "The best damn saloonkeeper you could be!"

–Joseph A. Deininger
General Manager
Charley's Crab
Beachwood, Ohio

As an educator, my fondest memory of Chuck was his indefatigable zeal for excellence in education. No risk was unthinkable if children's education could be improved.

–Sister Maureen A. Fay, O.P.
President
University of Detroit Mercy
Detroit, Michigan

*Nantucket Scallops, the sweetest, most delectable scallops, are in season from November to January.

SHERRY BUTTERED CAPE SCALLOPS
Recipe by Chef Loretto "Larry" Pagliara

Yield: 8 to 10 servings

1 pound scallops, Nantucket Cape Scallops*
2 tablespoons dry sack sherry
1/4 teaspoon paprika
1/4 teaspoon salt
1/3 cup Clarified Butter
1 cup all purpose flour

1. Place scallops on baking dish.

2. Season with salt.

3. Using a shaker, sprinkle with flour and paprika.

4. Evenly sprinkle sherry over scallops.

5. Brush scallops generously with Clarified Butter.

6. Place under broiler for 3 minutes or until golden in color.

To Serve:
Place scallops on a decorative tray with toothpicks and napkins on the side.

SALSA MEXICANA
Recipe by Chef Jim Blake

10 Plum tomatoes, ripe, diced
3 Jalapeñño peppers, minced
1 pound Spanish Onions, diced
6 tablespoons cilantro, chopped
3 limes, juiced
salt and pepper to taste

1. Combine all ingredients and stir.

2. May be made ahead; refrigerate until ready to use.

*M*y husband and I loved getting together with Chuck and Betty to play tennis in Traverse City. It was such an honor when Chuck asked me to work with him on his new cookbook. Their presence will really be missed in the community. They were two wonderful, generous people who touched the hearts of everyone they met, including us.

–Florine Mark
President
The WW Group Inc.
Farmington Hills,
Michigan

Salads

Chuck & Harold's, *Palm Beach, Florida. . . the great people-watching spot, with live entertainment and an open-air garden room for dining under the stars*

FRESH BUFFALO MOZZARELLA AND
    BEEFSTEAK TOMATO SALAD
SPINACH SALAD WITH HONEY MUSTARD
    DRESSING
BELGIAN ENDIVE SALAD
SALAD NIÇOISE
COBB SALAD
LOUIE DRESSING
GRILLED CHICKEN SALAD
CANNELLINI BEAN SALAD

Mozzarella is an Italian cheese originating from Campania, Italy. It is still made from buffalo milk and is a fresh cheese, springy and white.

*C*huck epitomized the pursuit of excellence in word and action. His desire and expectation of excellence was contagious to all who came in contact with him. Our sense of loss is tempered by the strength he engendered in all of us.

—James P. Gilan, ACSW
Executive Director
Blue Water Mental Health
Clinic
Fort Gratiot, Michigan

FRESH BUFFALO MOZZARELLA AND BEEFSTEAK TOMATO SALAD

Recipe developed for Chuck and Harold's, Palm Beach, Florida
A Simply Great Summer salad or entree!

Yield: 4 servings

2 pounds fresh buffalo mozzarella, must be fresh!
4 large tomatoes
1 medium red onion
4 fresh basil leaves, for garnish
6 ounces balsamic vinegar
2 ounces olive oil
1 shallot, chopped fine
1 tablespoon fresh basil, chopped fine

1. Whisk together in a small mixing bowl the balsamic vinegar and olive oil. Add the chopped shallots and 1 tablespoon fresh, chopped basil. Place in refrigerator.

2. Slice the fresh mozzarella into 12 medallions 1 inch thick.

3. Slice the tomatoes into 12 medallions 1 1/2 inches thick.

4. Place each alternately on the plate (there should be 3 of each on a plate).

5. Slice thin onion rings and place alongside the mozzarella and tomatoes. Add basil leaf for garnish.

6. Remove the balsamic vinaigrette from refrigerator. Whisk together well and ladle (2 ounces) evenly over the tomatoes, cheese and onions.

7. Serve immediately.

SPINACH SALAD
WITH HONEY MUSTARD DRESSING

Recipe by Chuck "Rocky" Rachwitz

Yield: 4 to 6 servings

2 pounds fresh spinach, cleaned
1/2 cup fresh mushrooms, sliced
1/4 cup red onion, julienne cut
20 pieces fresh orange sections
1 cup Honey Mustard Dressing (see page 8)

To Clean Spinach:

1. Remove stems and place spinach into a colander.

2. Place the colander into a large bowl of water, washing spinach well.

3. Drain and remove spinach from colander, place into a lettuce spinner to dry.

4. Prepare the Honey Mustard Dressing.

5. Place the spinach, mushrooms and onions in a bowl and toss well with the dressing.

6. Place an even amount of salad on 4 serving plates; neatly arrange 5 orange sections on each salad.

*O*ver many, many years, one of my dearest friends, who was one of the most vibrant figures on the Detroit scene, would call me early most mornings to discuss our respective plans for the day. Long ago we made a pact, that if possible, we'd try to set some time aside as often as possible to just have some fun out of life. For years, in addition to playing tennis and golf together, we traveled with our "male-bonding" buddies to run with the bulls in Pamplona, Spain, raft the rapids on the Deliverance river, attend the Masters golf tournaments, play the world championship golf courses in Ireland, and sail the Fort Lauderdale to Key West races. I sincerely miss the early morning calls from one of the greatest friends a guy could ever have. God bless and keep you, Chuck Muer, for all the great memories.

–Ray Lockhart
R. A. Lockhart & Co.
Detroit

I write to give thanks for having had the opportunity to share a friendship with Chuck Muer. We both served, for a number of years, on the board of trustees at the Interlochen Center for the Arts and I was always impressed by his quick mind, deep compassion and unselfishness. He was a man of absolute integrity and when I think of him I think of the Prophet Micah, who said: "He hath showed thee, O man, what is good; And what doth the Lord require of thee, But to do justly, and to love mercy, And to walk humbly with thy God?" Chuck Muer lived up to this admonition admirably and I will miss him very much, both as a friend and a colleague.

–Damon J. Keith
Circuit Judge
U.S. Court of Appeals
Detroit

BELGIAN ENDIVE SALAD
Recipe by Chef Chuck "Rocky" Rachwitz

Yield: 4 servings

1 head Bibb lettuce
2 heads Belgian Endive
8 mushrooms, washed and sliced thin
1 red pepper, 1/4 inch julienne cut
4 tablespoons walnuts, chopped
1/4 cup walnut oil
1/4 cup vegetable oil
1/4 cup blueberry vinegar
1 lemon, cut into wedges for garnish

1. Whisk together well the walnut oil, vegetable oil and blueberry vinegar. Chill.

2. Wash and separate lettuces. Do not break up leaves, keep whole.

3. Place the Bibb leaves along one side of the 4 plates evenly.

4. Place the leaves of the belgian endive crosswise, overlapping the Bibb leaves, then place the julienned red peppers inside the Belgian endive leaves.

5. Sprinkle the sliced mushrooms over the lettuce.

6. Whisk the vinaigrette together well and drizzle over the salad evenly. Top with the chopped walnuts and garnish with the lemon wedges.

SALAD NIÇOISE
Recipe by Chef Chuck "Rocky" Rachwitz

Yield: 4 servings

Four 5-ounce fresh tuna steaks
8 tomato wedges
16 Niçoise or Kalamata olives
1 cucumber, sliced 1/2 inch thick
1 small red or Vidalia onion, julienne cut
4 hard-boiled eggs, sliced
8 anchovy fillets
32 fresh green beans, blanched
8 red skin potatoes, boiled and chilled, sliced
2 red peppers, julienne cut 1/4 inch
1/2 cup Italian-style vinaigrette

Italian Vinaigrette:
1/4 cup balsamic vinegar
1/2 cup extra virgin olive oil
1 teaspoon dry oregano
1 teaspoon salt
1/4 teaspoon sugar
2 fresh basil leaves, chopped fine

1. Whisk together all ingredients well, refrigerate.

To Prepare Salad:
1. In a sauce pan bring water to a boil and cook the red skin potatoes for 20 minutes or until soft. Cool the potatoes completely under cold water, refrigerate. Cut the potatoes into 4 wedges, set aside.

2. Blanch the green beans in boiling water and chill under cold water.

*C*huck was an inspiration to all who knew him. As a restaurateur, family man and adventurer, he will remain always a role model and a man to admire and strive to be like.

–Keith Famie
Durango Grill
Royal Oak, Michigan

*W*e all know Chuck loved to fish. His salmon derby was especially close to his heart because he was helping people who truly needed help. He asked me to come up to St. Clair and we'd go out the week before the tournament and get the feeling of what it was like on the St. Clair River.

...

We caught nothing. Zip. Zero. Zilch. Poor Chuck was embarrassed. I didn't care because I was no fisherman. But he was upset because he wanted me to have a good time and we'd been shut out. But, as always, he found some humor in it all. For the following week here came a package to my home and it was from Chuck. He had mounted on a wooden board the smallest fish I had ever seen. It was guppy size and the inscription read: "1993 River Salmon Stakes. Media Fishing Tournament. Smallest Fish Caught."

The trophy hangs in my den to this day and never do I go in there that I do not look at it and think of Chuck. He is smiling. And so am I.

–Joe Falls
Sports Editor
The Detroit News

3. Place the green beans, potatoes, red peppers, and onions in a bowl with 1/3 cup of the vinaigrette and marinate for 2 hours.

4. Season the tuna steaks with salt and pepper, rub with olive oil and grill to medium rare (red inside meat).

5. Distribute the marinated mixture on 4 plates evenly. Arrange the sliced cucumber, tomato wedges and egg wedges around each plate.

6. Place the tuna steak in the center of the plate. Garnish with the olives and anchovy fillets. Top with the rest of the Italian vinaigrette.

COBB SALAD
Recipe by Chef Jim Blake

This is the original recipe from the Brown Derby Restaurant in Los Angeles.

Yield: 4 servings

*Mixed greens, 1/2 head each red leaf lettuce, Bibb and
   romaine
4 grilled chicken breasts (5 ounces each), diced
1 avocado (ripe), cubed, divide into 4 equal portions
1/2 cup cooked bacon, crumbled
1 cup blue cheese
1 cup Louie Dressing (See page 75)
1 cup red ripe tomatoes, diced*

1. Toss greens in one half cup of the Louie Dressing.

2. Divide into 4 servings, place in 4 bowls or plates.

3. Place 5 ounces of diced chicken in a neat row across the top of the greens.

4. Repeat in rows with the avocado, bacon, blue cheese and tomatoes.

5. Place the remaining Louie Dressing in a ramekin on the side to be used to top ingredients that were not previously tossed in the dressing.

*F*or over a year I searched the country for a restaurateur who would believe that the magnificent Pittsburgh & Lake Erie Railroad waiting room would make a successful major restaurant in Pittsburgh. I was told repeatedly: "The space is too large," "The acoustics are terrible," "The location is wrong," and, "No one wants to eat beside a railroad track."

A friend suggested that I try Engine House No. 5 in Columbus, Ohio, and, fortunately, I did. In just ten minutes there, I thought that the man who owns this is the man for Station Square, and I called Chuck Muer. He visited us and believed in the site and our mixed-use plan. ... The restaurant is now in the top fifty in gross sales in the nation. To us, today, fifteen years later, when we hear the happy sounds of people at the Gandy Dancer Oyster

Bar and the Grand Concourse Restaurant, we realize that his spirit, his profound vitality, and his affirmation of life are with us here in this fine business that he created and made a foundation for our revitalized city.

–Arthur P. Ziegler Jr.
President
Station Square
Pittsburgh

*C*huck Muer was a pro in the business and a leader in his field. His dynamic personality was a great asset for the restaurant business, the city of Detroit, and the numerous charities he supported. We will all miss him.

–Jimmy Schmidt
The Rattlesnake Club
Detroit

LOUIE DRESSING

Yield: 1 pint

1 3/4 cups mayonnaise
1/8 cup Heinz Chili Sauce
1 teaspoon red wine vinegar
1/2 teaspoon minced garlic

1. Combine all ingredients and mix well.

Salads

GRILLED CHICKEN SALAD
Recipe by Chef Jim Blake

Yield: 4 servings

Four 6-ounce boneless, skinless, chicken breasts
1 cup Honey Mustard Dressing (see page 8)
20 peeled orange sections (5 sections per salad)
8 peeled cantaloupe wedges (2 wedges per salad)
8 tomato wedges (2 wedges per salad)
8 leaves of red leaf lettuce
1 small bunch of grapes (red or green seedless)
1 apple, sliced (divide into 4 servings)
4 tablespoons walnuts, chopped (1 tablespoon per serving)

1. *Marinated Chicken Breasts*
   Four 6-ounce chicken breasts
   Four ounces Honey Mustard Dressing
   a. Pour the Honey Mustard Dressing over chicken breasts.
   b. Cover, refrigerate, marinate 2 to 4 hours

2. Grill chicken breasts on a preheated hot chargrill.

3. Refrigerate and cool the grilled chicken.

4. Place 2 leaves of red leaf lettuce in a wide rim pasta bowl or plate (per serving).

5. Slice each cooked chicken breast into 4 slices (1 breast per serving) and place it on the lettuce.

6. Brush with 1 ounce of Honey Mustard Dressing (per serving).

7. Arrange oranges, cantaloupe, tomatoes, apples and grapes around the outside of each bowl or plate.

8. Top with walnuts.

9. Drizzle remaining dressing over salad (1 ounce per serving).

We met Betty and Chuck many years ago when I became their pediatrician. From there, we went on to become warm friends. We traveled, fished, sailed and shared our celebrations together. His first big catering job was our daughter Bonnie's wedding. We could not ask for better or warmer friends. They added a dimension to our lives for which we will always be grateful.

–Doris & Dr. Irving Burton
Huntington Woods,
Michigan

Some years ago Chuck closed down Charley's Crab in Cleveland to do some remodeling. I had Marietta in class at the time. She told me one day that her dad would like to invite me and a guest to the reopening. Father Joe Zombor and I ... couldn't go until after my early evening class. When we arrived at the restaurant, we were told that Chuck and Marietta and Sue were downstairs waiting for us. What a host! After a warm greeting we sat down to sample some of the several special dishes Chuck ordered for all of us. ... Chuck made sure of this. After the main course Chuck introduced us to a number of different desserts. This is when Chuck, I think, smiled the most, because the little boy and little girl came out in all of us adults.

–Rev. Casey Bukala, S.J.
–Rev. JosephZombor, S. J.
John Carroll University
Cleveland

CANNELLINI BEAN SALAD
Recipe by Chef Peter Ashcraft

Yield: 6 servings

4 cups dried cannellini beans
2 tablespoons salt
1 gallon water
1/2 cup balsamic vinegar
1 cup extra virgin olive oil
1/2 tablespoon dried oregano
2 teaspoons salt
1/2 teaspoon sugar
3 large fresh basil leaves, chopped
36 green beans, cooked al dente and cooled
2 large, very ripe tomatoes, diced medium
1/2 small red or Vidalia onion, fine julienne cut
36 arugula leaves, washed

1. In a heavy bottom pot, place water, 2 tablespoons salt, dried beans and bring to a boil, then simmer, covered until beans are tender, about 1 1/2 to 2 hours.

2. When beans are tender, strain and lay out on a sheet tray to cool.

3. To prepare vinaigrette, vigorously whisk together the balsamic vinegar, olive oil, oregano, salt, sugar and chopped basil, set aside.

4. Arrange arugula in a flower design around perimeter of 6 salad plates, or on 1 large platter for buffet or picnic service, allowing an empty space in center.

5. Toss cannellini beans, green beans, and tomatoes in vinaigrette and place in the center of each plate/platter. Top with julienne red or Vidalia onions.

Pasta

Charley's Crab, Jupiter, Florida . . . open and airy overlooking the Jupiter
Yacht Harbor and the Intracoastal Waterway

SMOKED SALMON FETTUCCINE
LINGUINE WITH RED CLAM SAUCE
PENNE PASTA WITH SMOKED CHICKEN
TOMATO BASIL CREAM
ARTICHOKE PASTA POULETTE
SCROD PASTA PESCA

Pastas

Al Dente (To the Tooth). Chuck Muer loved his pasta cooked this way. It is an Italian expression indicating the correct degree of cooking for pasta, which must be removed from the heat and drained while it is still firm enough to bite into.

The best smoked salmon comes from fish that has been recently smoked. It is therefore best to buy from a store with high turnover. The best is Scottish smoked salmon, which has a tender smoky flavor. Whereas Norwegian smoked salmon has a more pronounced flavor.

SMOKED SALMON FETTUCCINE
Recipe by Chef Loretto "Larry" Pagliara

Yield: 4 servings

8 ounces smoked salmon, sliced thin, cut to 1-inch wide.
1 cup White Clam Sauce (see page 11)
3 cups heavy cream
4 egg yolks
1/2 cup frozen peas (defrost at room temperature)
1 pound white fettuccine

1. Prepare the White Clam Sauce.

2. Cook the fettuccine in 4 quarts of salted boiling water until tender(al dente), drain and toss with 1 teaspoon olive oil. Cover and keep warm.

3. Meanwhile whisk together the heavy cream and egg yolks. Set aside.

4. Mix the White Clam Sauce well just prior to using. Place the White Clam Sauce into a large teflon coated saute pan. Heat the sauce until very hot.

5. Add the smoked salmon to the White Clam Sauce and cook for 1 minute on medium heat.

6. Slowly add the heavy cream mixture and the peas. Heat, but do not boil. Simmer until sauce is slightly thickened.

To Serve:
1. Toss the cooked pasta with the sauce and evenly distribute the smoked salmon, peas and pasta onto 4 plates.

LINGUINE WITH RED CLAM SAUCE
Recipe by Chef Loretto "Larry" Pagliara

This dish has been heralded as a classic favorite of our guests for more than twenty years. So simple, so great to eat!

Yield: 4 servings

1 cup olive oil
1 large garlic clove, finely diced
1 1/4 cups hot water
5 tablespoons clam base
3 tablespoons fresh parsley, finely chopped
1 cup Provençal sauce (see page 10)
1 pound linguine pasta (preferably fresh linguine)
3 cups fresh clams, preferably cherrystones or littlenecks, shucked, chopped (see page 16).

1. Blend garlic and olive oil in a food processor until emulsified.

2. Place garlic mixture in a saucepan and heat gently.

3. While garlic mixture is heating, whisk together clam base and hot water to make the clam broth.

4. When garlic mixture is hot, remove from burner and add the parsley. Quickly pour clam broth into garlic mixture to make the clam sauce. Set aside.

5. Prepare the Provençal sauce. (see page 10).

6. Bring 4 quarts salted water to a boil. Add pasta and cook until tender (al dente). Strain and keep warm.

We loved Betty for her honesty, her laughter and her thoughtfulness. Betty and I enjoyed playing in golf club invitationals for more than a dozen years. Nineteen ninety-two was a great year. We won first place at St. Clair Country Club and Port Huron Golf Club.

–Judy Moore
Port Huron, Michigan

Fresh pasta is made by small businesses or in the home. It cooks much faster than dried noodles, so should be watched carefully as not to overcook.

*C*huck Muer's bright smile and captivating flamboyant way with both restaurant patrons and staff has always been the hallmark and standard for the Chuck Muer restaurant chain. In my almost twenty years on legal counsel to the company, I was constantly in awe of Chuck's forte to lead and teach by example. His personality lives on in the restaurant's personality.

–Gary A. Taback
Sommers, Schwartz, Silver
& Schwartz
Southfield, Michigan

7. While pasta is cooking, transfer clam sauce to a sauté pan and gently cook the fresh clams in it. Add the Provençal Sauce and simmer until hot or 4 minutes.

To Serve:

1. Toss the pasta with the red clam sauce, making sure that all the noodles are evenly coated with the sauce.

2. Divide among 4 dinner plates and serve immediately.

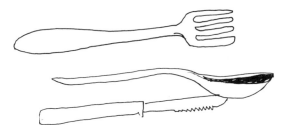

PENNE PASTA WITH SMOKED CHICKEN, TOMATO BASIL CREAM
Recipe created for Chuck & Harold's, Palm Beach, Florida

Yield: 4 servings

1/4 cup Casino Butter (see page 12)
1 cup Provençal Sauce (see page 10)
1 cup heavy cream
2 egg yolks
2 tablespoons fresh basil, julienne (cut into thin matchstick strips)
4 tablespoons tomato, fresh, chopped
1 pound penne pasta, uncooked
2 pounds chicken breast, smoked, sliced 1/4 inch thick

To Smoke Chicken:
2 cups water
1/4 cup honey
2 tablespoons kosher salt
2 tablespoons sugar

1. Combine water, honey, salt, and sugar, mix well.

2. Add chicken, let marinate for 30 minutes.

3. Drain chicken, place in smoker for 6 minutes.

4. Cool and slice.

To Cook Penne Pasta:
Bring 4 quarts salted water to a boil. Add pasta and cook until tender (al dente). Strain, toss with one teaspoon olive oil and keep warm. This will prevent the pasta from sticking together.

When I think of Chuck, which I do fondly and often, I think of: getting every color of Charley's Crab bow tie so I can practice my new-found skill of tying a bow tie; how the matronly elevator operator at the Drake Hotel in Chicago wouldn't let him up without his room key after 11 P.M. (which he forgot!) and I got a midnight call from security to be his character witness; how lovingly he spoke of his family; what a wonderful, fun-loving and warm person he was and how his absence leaves a void.

–Cindy Estis Green
Driving Revenue
Rockville, Maryland

1. In a hot sauté pan, combine Casino Butter and Provençal Sauce.

2. Add chicken, heat for 1 minute, add cooked pasta, tossing to coat well.

3. Combine egg yolks and cream together, mix well. Add to pasta, bring to a boil slowly, and simmer on low for 2 minutes.

4. Add tomato, basil and toss thoroughly; divide into 4 pasta bowls, and serve immediately.

When I think of Chuck Muer, I can't help but smile. I'll never forget the Shorthills, New Jersey, grand opening dinner way back when. ... I was so impressed with Chuck's hand-tied bow tie that the appetizer included a lesson for all the guests at our table on how to tie a bow tie so that the crab was displayed perfectly in the center of the knot. ... Every time someone comments on a great tie or asks why I always wear them, I smile and say it's in honor of a dear friend, Chuck Muer. It's pretty impressive when a man has an impact on how you dress for work.

–Debbie Estis Trainor
Driving Revenue
Rockville, Maryland

ARTICHOKE PASTA POULETTE
Recipe by Chef Loretto "Larry" Pagliara

Yield: 4 servings

Four 6-ounce skinless chicken breasts
1 cup artichoke hearts, quartered
1 cup Casino Butter (see page 12)
2 cups Provencal Sauce (see page 10)
1/2 cup pitted black olives, sliced
20 ounces linguine noodles, precooked and cooled

To Cook Linguine:
Bring 4 quarts salted water to a boil. Add pasta and cook until tender (al dente). Strain and cool. Add a small amount of vegetable or olive oil to the linguine noodles and toss gently, this will prevent them from sticking.

1. Cook chicken breasts on a grill and cut into strips.

2. Place Casino Butter in a large sauté pan or pot and heat until melted.

3. Add Provencal Sauce and simmer for 3 minutes.

4. Add chicken and artichokes. Cover and cook 3 minutes.

5. Add linguine and olives and mix well.

To Serve:
Toss the cooked linguine with the prepared sauce. Divide equally among 4 plates and serve immediately. Garnish with freshly grated Reggiano Parmesan cheese.

When I think of Chuck and Betty my thoughts go to good humor, good food, and most of all, their genuine and consistent concern for others, which so often stimulated them into action on behalf of the group. My life was enriched by our friendship. Chuck, I can hear your laughter. I will always remember that infectious laugh.

–Francis X. Walton, Ph.D.
John Carroll University
Class of '59
Columbia, South Carolina

Reggiano Parmesan is an Italian cheese made from skimmed cow's milk. Reggiano Parmesan is manufactured from April 15 to November 11 in the province of Parma, Italy. It takes at least one year to mature and is used principally grated in pastas.

I immediately recognized Chuck's intense and intellectual nature when we first met as competitors in the data processing industry in the 1960s. Over the years, his intensity never waned, and his sincerity and strength influenced everyone who knew him. His integrity and ceaseless quest for knowledge is sorely missed by all.

–Ed Cherney
Bloomfield Hills
Michigan

Chuck Muer, a man bigger than life and a heart to match. I will never forget the kindness he expressed to me in my early years as a stockholder. He will be surely missed.

–Robert J. Barrett, CLU
The Penn Mutual Life
Insurance Company
Southfield, Michigan

SCROD PASTA PESCA
Vision from Chuck Muer

Chuck Muer's favorite fish was Boston Scrod. Chuck not only enjoyed scrod's flaky white meat but felt that "amateur" fish eaters would love this dish.

Yield: 4 servings

2 pounds skinless fresh scrod, uncooked, sliced 1/4-inch thick and 1 1/2 inches long
1 cup White Clam Sauce (see page 11)
1 cup Casino Butter (see page 12)
1 cup Provençal Sauce (see page 10)
4 tablespoons peas (frozen, thawed at room temperature)
Five 5-ounce portions linguine, whole wheat

To Cook Linguine:
Bring 4 quarts salted water to a boil. Add the linguine and cook until tender (al dente). Strain and keep warm. Toss with a small amount of vegetable or olive oil to prevent the pasta from sticking together.

1. Prepare ahead of time: White Clam Sauce, Casino Butter and Provençal Sauce.

2. Place White Clam Sauce into a pan, add scrod, cover and cook for 4 minutes.

3. Add casino butter, provencal sauce and peas, simmer for 5 minutes on medium heat.

4. Add cooked linguine to sauce and toss lightly.

5. Place linguine on 4 individual plates and distribute remaining sauce evenly over pasta.

Pastas

Entrées

Grand Concourse, Pittsburgh, Pennsylvania . . . Pennsylvania & Lake
Erie Railroad terminal restored to its turn-of-the-century grandeur on the
Monongahela River with a breathtaking view of downtown Pittsburgh

SWORDFISH PICATA
SHRIMP AND CHICKEN DIJON
THE SHAFT BBQ BABY BACK RIBS
TEXAS BARBECUE WHITEFISH WITH
     BRAISED BLACK AND WHITE BEANS
SEAFOOD SAUTÉ
FISH VERA CRUZ
SALMON CAKES
MARTHA'S VINEYARD RASPBERRY CHICKEN
CEDAR PLANKED COHO SALMON WITH
     MUSTARD-TARRAGON GLAZE WITH
     GRILLED VEGETABLES AND ROASTED
     POTATOES
SHRIMP STUFFED WITH CRABMEAT
BLACKENED YELLOWFIN TUNA
BOUILLABAISSE
PAELLA
BRAISED LAMB SHANKS
SAUTEED SKATE WINGS WITH CAPERS
     AND BROWN BUTTER

Chuck converted our business relationship into a friendship. Long past our work together was finished–all of which he criticized vigorously–he maintained his friendship. Chuck was often impossible, demanding, unreasonable, brilliant, courageous, creative, infuriating and, God forgive me, once in a while even wrong. His loyalty was wonderful, his ideas and cares wide-ranging and passionate. Always straight and right or wrong without malice, never coy. His camaraderie was joyful and lusty, and I shall miss him terribly.

–Richard Bloch
Architect
New York City

When cooking the picata, be sure to use a clean pan at all times.

SWORDFISH PICATA
Created for Charley's Crab in Troy

Yield: 4 servings

2 pounds fresh swordfish, skinless
1/2 cup peanut oil
Salt to season
2 cups flour for dusting
1 1/2 cups fresh mushrooms, sliced thin
1/2 cup dry sack sherry
2 fresh lemons
1 1/2 tablespoons chopped parsley, for garnish

1. Slice the skinless swordfish into medallions 3 inches in diameter and approximately 1/4-inch thick (3 pieces to weigh 8 ounces, or 12 pieces in all).

2. Place the peanut oil in teflon coated sauté pan and get hot. Add salt to season.

3. Dust the swordfish medallions lightly with flour and place in hot oil. Allow to sauté until golden in color. Turn over medallions and cook until golden in color.

4. Add the juice of 2 fresh lemons and the dry sack sherry.

5. Remove the swordfish medallions from the sauté pan and place 3 medallions on each plate.

6. Add the mushroom slices to the sauté pan, mix with the dry sack and lemon sauce for 1 minute.

7. Ladle the mushroom sauce evenly over all 4 entrees using all the sauce. Sprinkle with the chopped parsley.

8. Serve immediately.

SHRIMP AND CHICKEN DIJON
Recipe by Chef Loretto "Larry" Pagliara

Yield: 4 servings

24 large shrimp, peeled, deveined and butterflied
2 pounds chicken breast, skin on
4 cups Rice Pilaf (see recipe on page 26)
8 bamboo skewers
1 bunch fresh parsley, chopped fine

Mustard Sauce:
1 1/2 cups mayonnaise
1 1/4 cups Dijon mustard, preferably Grey Poupon
1 teaspoon dry mustard
3 tablespoons fresh lemon juice

Dijon Sauce:
1 cup heavy whipping cream
1 egg yolk
1 tablespoon Grey Poupon mustard
2 teaspoon Worcestershire sauce
1/4 cup Casino Butter (see page 12)

1. Remove skin of chicken breasts and cut into 16 equal pieces. Thaw the shrimp properly, peel, devein and butterfly the shrimp by taking a paring knife and slicing halfway through the back of the shrimp. Leave the tail on.

2. Place the shrimp and chicken on 8 skewers, starting and ending with shrimp. There should be 3 shrimp and 2 chicken on each skewer.

3. Place the mayonnaise, Dijon mustard, dry mustard and lemon juice in a bowl and mix together well.

Ginny and I have many fond memories, including those cross-country ski outings, which started at Chuck and Betty's house but always seemed to end at the River Crab with hot drinks and a sampling of some new seafood concoction. Of course, the many pre-Salmon Stakes dinners with good food, good wine and great friends, as well as the sometimes successful but always enjoyable Salmon Stakes Tournament itself, will forever be remembered. We can never forget Betty's ever present smile, her many humorous stories about Chuck, or her knack for always knowing the latest joke going around. But I guess I'll cherish most the memory of those early summer morning phone calls when a much too cheery voice at the other end of the line would say, "Hey, Jake, it's Chuck Muer, let's go fishing!"

–Jake Hirt
The Bruss Company
Hamtramck, Michigan

What sticks in the minds of all of us–family, friends and acquaintances–is that Chuck and Betty led a life that was fun-filled, adventuresome and meaningful. And what sticks in the minds of those of us who love our community is that the Muer name has meant so much to our business, social and cultural life. Detroit has been in the hearts of the Muers for three generations. The Muers have been in the hearts of Detroiters just as long. There is no greater legacy for two people to leave.

–U.S. Senator Carl Levin
Michigan

4. Brush each kabob with the mustard sauce, place on a sheet tray and marinate in refrigerator for 1 hour.

5. Prepare the Rice Pilaf recipe.

6. Mix together in a bowl the heavy cream, egg yolk, mustard and Worcestershire, and set aside.

7. Melt the Casino Butter in a sauté pan, add the heavy cream mixture and warm slightly. Remove from stove. Keep warm until ready to use.

8. Preheat chargrill and oil well before starting to avoid sticking.

9. Place skewers on chargrill, cook on both sides for 5 minutes or until done.

To Serve:
1. Place 1 cup of cooked Rice Pilaf on each plate.

2. Place 2 skewers on top of rice, and ladle the warm Dijon sauce over the skewers. Garnish with the chopped parsley.

Entrées

THE SHAFT BBQ BABY BACK RIBS
Recipe by Chef Loretto "Larry" Pagliara

*This classic dish was developed in the late 1960s for
The Shaft Restaurant in Aspen, Colorado. Chuck Muer, while
out on a visit, fell in love with this then-small mining town.
We operated this restaurant for almost twenty years before shut-
ting its doors in the mid 80s. As you probably know, Aspen is
now known for its year round outdoor sporting and celebrity
watching.*

Yield: 6 to 8 servings

*6 pounds pork baby back spare ribs, 6 to 7 ribs depending on
    weight (approximately 12 ounces each)*
4 cups Barbecue Sauce (see recipe below)
3 cups water

Barbecue Sauce:
8 cups Open Pit Barbecue Sauce
1 1/4 cups ketchup
1 tablespoon Wrights Liquid Smoke
1 fresh lemon
3/4 cup water
1 tablespoon salt
1 teaspoon pepper
1/2 cup honey

1. Place all Barbecue Sauce ingredients into a large mixing
   bowl, utilize the 3/4 cup of water to wash out the BBQ
   sauce bottles, mix well. Set aside.

2. To prepare the ribs, trim off any silver skin and excess fat
   from the slab. Score along bone end, approximately 4
   cuts.

3. Place 3 cups of water into the bottom of a
   4-inch deep roasting pan.

Chuck Muer was, as
the old song goes,
"One Happy Fella," who
became a dynamic leader,
an entrepreneur extraordi-
naire, a creative thinker
and visionary, a builder of
dreams, fun loving, a risk
taker, generous and helpful
to others. He was a man
who, with a positive men-
tal attitude, always enjoyed
being on the "cutting
edge" as he lived life to the
fullest in all his endeavors.

—Roger E. Jacobi
President Emeritus
Interlochen Center for the
Arts
Naples, Florida

4. Dip each rib into the large bowl of Barbecue Sauce making sure they are well covered.

5. Line the ribs in the pan by placing the bone down, overlapping the edges of the ribs.

6. Pour the leftover sauce (4 cups) evenly over the ribs.

7. Cover with saran wrap and allow 12 hours to marinate.

8. Remove the saran wrap and cover with aluminum foil.

9. Place in a preheated 350 degree oven for 1 1/2 to 2 hours. Baste ribs every 20 minutes. Ribs must be turned at least once while cooking. The ribs are done when meat is a white grey.

10. Remove the ribs from the roaster and place on a deep tray.

11. Place the roaster on medium heat and boil sauce. Skim off any fat. Set sauce aside.

12. Preheat chargrill on high.

13. Dip the ribs into the precooked sauce and place on chargrill to heat for 7 to 10 minutes. Turn ribs at least once.

14. Remove ribs, place on a decorative platter to serve.

15. The extra sauce is great for dipping.

While working with Chuck on education reform, we often confronted opponents of change. He would share with them his view of the status quo: "The more you do of what you are doing, the more you'll get of what you already have." Many then saw differently the need for change. That insight remains for me a frequently used reminder of his fundamentals-based vision and of his great zest for making things better than they are.

–John M. Amberger
President, Metropolitan
Affairs Corporation
Detroit

TEXAS BARBECUE WHITEFISH
WITH BRAISED BLACK AND WHITE BEANS
Recipe by Chef Chuck "Rocky" Rachwitz

Yield: 4 servings

2 pounds fresh whitefish fillets, 8 ounces each
Braised black and white beans (see page 123)

Texas BBQ Sauce:
1 1/2 cups orange juice concentrate
1/2 cup soy sauce
1 cup ketchup
3/4 cup molasses
4 teaspoons worcestershire sauce
2 teaspoons tabasco
1 1/2 cups chili sauce
2 tablespoons Dijon mustard
2 cloves garlic, chopped fine
2 tablespoons fresh lemon juice
1/2 cup chicken broth
2 teaspoons salt
1 teaspoon red pepper flakes

1. In a large bowl mix together all the ingredients for the Texas BBQ Sauce.

2. Place the four 8 ounce white fish fillets in a deep casserole dish. Pour the BBQ sauce over the fish and marinate overnight or 24 hours.

3. Place the whitefish fillets on a sheet pan and broil on medium heat until the BBQ sauce is well caramelized, about 12 to 15 minutes.

To Serve:
Place each fillet on a plate and serve as a great vegetable accompaniment the Braised Black and White Beans. *(see page 123)*

When I first met Chuck in the late sixties he was in charge of the F & B concession at the Hotel Pontchartrain. ... I'll never forget a marathon two-day-and-night session with Chuck, where after deciding on a Bohemian uniform for cocktail waitresses, redesigning the menu to be written on the score of La Boheme, an artist's palette for a cocktail tray, and so forth, I said, "We need the ambiance to be complete with French prints to signal the period of the opera theme in Paris." Chuck got up and started to leave the room. I said, "Where are you going?" Chuck replied, "To Paris, to buy some authentic prints." Attention to detail and concept development was an absolute strength that comes with a feeling about what people want, and Chuck really had that in spades! We'll miss him and his beautiful wife.

–Peter J. Nunez
Executive Vice President,
Syn-Cronamics Inc.
Englewood Cliffs,
New Jersey

Be careful not to over-cook the scallops and crabmeat as they will become tough.

*I*n the many years I was blessed in knowing Chuck Muer, I got into the habit of thinking of him as a man who was always searching. As we all know now, he was a man who searched for what was best for Betty and the children, what was best for the schools, what was best for and what led to his great achievements in business. So I have great faith that Betty and Chuck ended their searching safely in the arms of their Heavenly Father.

–Rev. Malcolm Carron, S.J. Detroit

SEAFOOD SAUTÉ
Recipe by Chef Chuck "Rocky" Rachwitz

Yield: 4 servings

1 pound fresh Nantucket cape scallops
1/2 pound Alaskan King Crab meat, large dice
16 large shrimp, peeled, deveined and butterflied
8 tablespoons extra virgin olive oil
8 tablespoons Casino Butter (see page 12)
8 tablespoons dry sack sherry
2 tablespoons sliced almonds, toasted for garnish
1 cup all purpose flour
2 cups Rice Pilaf (see page 26)

1. Prepare the Casino Butter.

2. Prepare the Rice Pilaf.

3. Place olive oil into a hot sauté pan.

4. Thaw the shrimp properly. Peel, devein and butterfly the shrimp by taking a paring knife and slicing halfway through the back of the shrimp. Leave the tail on.

5. Dust the shrimp with flour, place in hot oil and sauté until half cooked.

6. Add the scallops, crabmeat and sauté until cooked. Add the Casino Butter and dry sack sherry. Mix well.

7. Place the cooked Rice Pilaf on 4 plates and distribute the seafood evenly over the rice. Garnish with toasted almonds.

Entrées

FISH VERA CRUZ
Recipe by Chef Jim Blake

This is a traditional recipe from the southern part of Mexico. In Mexico it is called "Huachinango," which is a whole 1 1/2-pound Red Snapper that is deep fried and served with the Vera Cruz Sauce. This recipe has been modified for American tastes, less spicy and using filets instead of whole fish.

Yield: 4 servings

Four 8-ounce filets of whitefish (or grouper, snapper, halibut, sea bass)

Vera Cruz Sauce:
One 28-ounce can whole, peeled tomatoes (take each tomato, one by one, place it in the palm of your hand and close your fingers around the tomato; this will break it up and ready it for use)
1/4 cup yellow onions, diced
1/4 cup green pepper, diced
2 tablespoons garlic, minced
1 tablespoon capers
3 tablespoons stuffed green olives with pimiento, chopped coarsely
3 tablespoons cilantro (fresh coriander)
1 teaspoon jalapeno pepper, minced
2 tablespoons olive oil
Salt & pepper to taste

1. Place olive oil in heated sauté pan.

2. Add garlic, onions and peppers.

3. Sauté until onions are translucent.

4. Add tomatoes, capers, olives and jalapeno pepper.

We were dining at Charley's Crab one evening with two other couples and did not know Chuck Muer was at the table behind us. He saw me and came over to say hello. I introduced him to all the people at our table and he proceeded to tell them how wonderful a person I was as I tried to tell them all about his many accomplishments. That was Chuck Muer. Always building up someone else instead of himself. ... I'll never forget the night ... I told him I was changing coffee companies and asked him to give me a comparison trial with my new company. His response was, change the coffee. I buy from you because I trust you.

–Charles Litt
Cadillac Coffee
Detroit

*I*t was in the early years of the Muer Corporation that my wife, Evie, and I saw Chuck and Betty more often.... I had a chance to write some humorous letters about the stockholders detailing their outrageous behavior, ficti-tious, of course. Chuck enjoyed reading them to liven up their annual meet-ings. When we had dinner together ... I was impressed with Chuck's knowledge of oenology, the study of wines. Chuck was always a go-getter and I can see how he attacked the ocean with the same vigor that he challenged the restau-rant business. Sadly enough, the ocean proved to be unconquerable, but his success in the latter was unprecedented. We will always remember Chuck and Betty Muer, two delightful people whom we had the privilege of know-ing.

–Dick Iliff
West Palm Beach
Florida

5. Bring to a boil, reduce heat and simmer 20 minutes.

6. Remove from heat, add cilantro, salt and pepper.

7. Grill, broil or bake fish.

8. Place 2 ounces of Vera Cruz Sauce on a warm serving plate.

9. Place cooked fish on top of the sauce.

10. Add rice and vegetable to complete this entree.

SALMON CAKES
Recipe by Chef Loretto "Larry" Pagliara

Yield: 4 servings
8 cakes

1 1/2 pound salmon poached, cooled and broken up after
  removing the skin and bones.
1 egg beaten
5 tablespoons mayonnaise
1 tablespoon fresh parsley, chopped
2 teaspoons Worcestershire sauce
1 teaspoon prepared mustard
1 teaspoon salt
1/4 teaspoon white pepper
1/2 cup bread crumbs
2 tablespoons olive oil or melted butter

Serve with Mustard Sauce (see page 9)—OR—Cajun
Remoulade Sauce (see page 6)

1. Place salmon in a bowl.
2. In a separate bowl, mix together egg, mayonnaise, parsley, Worcestershire sauce, mustard, salt and pepper.
3. Gently fold bread crumbs into salmon with a rubber spatula.
4. Fold egg mixture into salmon mixture without breaking up the meat. Refrigerate mixture 1 hour.
5. Form mixture into 8 cakes, approximately 2 1/2 inches wide and 3/4 inch thick.
6. Place cakes on a foil-covered baking sheet that has been brushed lightly with olive oil or melted butter. Cakes may be refrigerated until ready to broil and serve.
7. Broil cakes for 10 to 12 minutes or until golden brown. Serve with either the Mustard Sauce or the Cajun Remoulade Sauce *(see page 6)*.

Chuck always said he served his friends in his restaurants for over twenty-five years and he also bought his products from his friends. He ran his business like he did his life, with his warm heart and his fine mind. ... The best advice I ever received was when I asked Chuck what to name my new company. He said, "Call it Steve Connolly Seafood Co. People like to do business with people not names." He was sure right on that score. The last time I saw Betty she was at her loveliest and happiest. It was at the grand opening of Big Fish. She was so proud and excited about the great decorating job she had done. It was sensational. ... Whenever we had a board meeting Chuck would make it an event with his great wit, charm and visionary ideas. I miss him very much and think of both him and Betty with love every day of my life.

–Steve Connolly
Steve Connolly Seafood
Co. Inc.
Boston

Although Chuck rowed briefly during his high school days, his love of the sport remained with him. He decorated several of his restaurants with our retired racing boats. He donated funds to purchase a shell bearing the name of Charley's Crab. Chuck's support and generosity at our annual fund-raiser, held at the River Crab and Charley's Crab, will be missed. Row on Chuck.

–Denne Osgood
President, Friends of
Detroit Rowing
Lathrup Village, Michigan

*M*r. Restaurateur, Chuck Muer, your special friendship brought great cheer;
you'll always be remembered, whether here or near.

–Jerry L. Hill
Chief Executive Officer
Bill Knapp's
Battle Creek, Michigan

MARTHA'S VINEYARD RASPBERRY CHICKEN
Recipe by Chef Jim Blake

Yield: 4 servings

Spicy Raspberry Glaze:
1/2 pound raspberry jelly or jam (found in most grocery stores)
2 ounces chicken broth
1/2 teaspoon cayenne pepper
2 ounces Maple-Raspberry Vinaigrette Dressing (see page 21)

1. Combine all ingredients in a saucepan.

2. Bring to a boil, reduce heat, simmer 15 minutes.

3. Cool mixture and hold for use.

Raspberry Chicken:
Four 8-ounce (each) boneless, skinless chicken breasts
1/2 cup Maple-Raspberry Vinaigrette (see page 21)
4 teaspoons pine nuts, toasted
4 ounces Rice Pilaf
4 ounces vegetable du jour
1 cup Spicy Raspberry Glaze (see recipe above)

1. Prepare Maple Raspberry Dressing, pour vinaigrette evenly over chicken breasts and marinate for 2 hours.

2. Grill chicken breasts. After turning once brush with 1 ounce of the Spicy Raspberry Glaze on each breast and continue to cook.

3. When chicken is done place on a plate and brush each breast with an additional 1 ounce of Spicy Glaze.

4. Top with 1 teaspoon of toasted pine nuts (per serving).

 5. Add rice and vegetable.

Entrées ———————————————— *105*

CEDAR PLANKED COHO SALMON WITH MUSTARD-TARRAGON GLAZE AND GRILLED VEGETABLES AND ROASTED POTATOES
Recipe by Chef Jim Blake

Yield: 4 servings

Plank cooking is one of the oldest methods of fish cookery. In the old days the fish were secured to planks and cooked leaning at a 70 degree angle next to a fire. Shad and shad roe in the East, whitefish and other fresh water species in the Midwest, and salmon in the Northwest. The planks are the cooking utensils and the plates! This adds a nice soft, smoky flavor to the fish and is a striking service vehicle. You can have cedar planks cut at any lumber yard or order planks designed for cooking. Prior to the first usage, brush boards with good olive oil and bake for about 20 minutes in a 275 degree oven.

This has become a "signature" dish at Chuck Muer restaurants.

Mustard-Tarragon Glaze:
2 tablespoons butter
2 tablespoons extra virgin olive oil (plus a little more to brush on plank and fish)
1 teaspoon prepared mustard
1/2 teaspoon Dijon mustard
1 tablespoon chopped fresh tarragon

1. Melt butter, being careful not to let it get hot enough to separate.

2. Whisk in olive oil, mustards and tarragon, set aside.

From nights in eighth grade when Chuck and I "cruised" on our bikes, through our University of Detroit High School Class of '55 to evenings at River Crab, Chuck defined the word vitality. He always knew that anything worth having is worth working for..

–John Diebel
Grosse Pointe Park,
Michigan

Also an excellent glaze for grilled fish and chicken dishes.

It was a beautiful sunny day in downtown Munich, June 1982. I was a "resource" with the Young Presidents' Organization University. ... My assignment was to speak on corporate art, and a "Sketch with Olendorf" course. At the end of three outside sketch sessions, one new art student did much better than anyone else. He won the "Best of Class" award and joined me, with his wife, at dinner. It was Chuck and Betty Muer. ... Since then we became good friends and Chuck always wanted to join me on one of my art assignments in Europe—but last-minute changes always got in the way. Chuck told me he hoped to get into sketching more when he could relax more, away from the business. ... I was happy to have known them and the whole Muer clan!

–Bill Olendorf
Olendorf Art Promo Inc.
Chicago

Cedar Planked Coho Salmon:
4 cedar wooden planks
Four 8- to 10-ounce coho salmon (dressed with head and tail intact)
8 redskin or other small potatoes, cut in halves and roasted
4 whole carrots, blanched and charred under the broiler
4 strips red pepper, oiled and charred under the broiler
4 strips green pepper, oiled and charred under the broiler
4 strips zucchini, julienned, oiled and charred under the broiler
4 strips yellow squash, julienned, oiled and charred under the broiler
salt and pepper

1. Roast potato halves in a 375 degree oven for 20 minutes or until soft.

2. Brush cedar planks lightly with a little olive oil, set open fillets on planks, flesh side up. Lightly brush the top of the fillet with olive oil and season with the salt and pepper.

3. Place in a 375 degree oven for 10 to 12 minutes.

4. Remove planks from oven and carefully drain off any excess olive oil. Brush generously with the Mustard-Tarragon Glaze, arrange grilled vegetables around fish, garnish with potatoes and serve on planks.

SHRIMP STUFFED WITH CRABMEAT
Recipe by Chef Loretto "Larry" Pagliara

This is the most popular dish at Big Fish in Dearborn, Michigan.

Yield: 4 servings

16 large shrimp, peeled, deveined and butterflied
2 cups Crabmeat Stuffing (see page 29)
2 tablespoons Parmesan cheese, grated
2 tablespoons butter, melted
1 teaspoon kosher salt

1. Peel and devein shrimp, clean well. Leaving tails on, split down the center from the back side, cutting almost but not completely through. The two halves are then opened flat to resemble a butterfly shape; this will create a well butterflied shrimp to hold the stuffing.

2. Season shrimp with salt.

3. Place 2 tablespoons of crabmeat stuffing on butterflied shrimp, covering entire surface.

4. Sprinkle with Parmesan cheese, and drizzle melted butter over the top of each shrimp.

5. Bake in moderate oven at 350 degrees for approximately 5 minutes or until browned to a golden color.

The shrimp must be free of water and dry.

*T*he first time I ever had contact with Chuck was over the phone. ... Chuck was looking to fill the position of director of marketing for his company. ... Our first encounter lasted only about five minutes. ... He simply asked what would be the earliest time I could get to Detroit to meet face-to-face. ... When I arrived ... I found Chuck to be unpretentious, warm, hospitable and genuinely concerned about me as a person. ... I learned that he believed that his front-line managers and employees were the most important people in his organization. ... Other leaders often make claims similar to this. It was apparent to me that he truly believed and practiced this philosophy. ...

Chuck invited me to return again with my wife, Janet. ... He wanted to make sure that the chemistries were right for all, including my wife. Plus, he was the type of individual who was decisive and moved quickly when something was important to him and needed to get done. ... The entire [interview] process took only about three weeks. Most organizations typically interview prospects for three months or longer, and still know far less about the individual than Chuck learned about me in a fraction of the time. Even though I have long since left the C. A. Muer Corporation, I have great admiration and fond memories of Chuck, Betty, their family and the organization.

–R. Jay Olson
VP, Marketing and
Account Services
Phoenix Marketing Group
Inc.
Brookfield, Wisconsin

BLACKENED YELLOWFIN TUNA
Recipe by Chef Chuck "Rocky" Rachwitz

Yield: 4 servings

Four 8-ounce yellowfin tuna steaks
4 tablespoons Cajun Seasoning (see page 7)
4 teaspoons butter
Salt & pepper to taste
2 tablespoons butter, melted

1. Grab that cast iron skillet from way in the back of the cupboard, dust off the cobwebs and put it on the stove on high heat. After about 10 minutes, when skillet is smoking hot, we are ready to begin.

2. Brush each tuna steak with the melted butter and evenly season with salt and pepper. Sprinkle evenly with the Cajun spice mixture (oops, turn on the exhaust fan full blast before the smoke detector goes off!).

3. Place the tuna steaks in the hot skillet. After about 2 minutes flip it over and cook 2 minutes more; top each steak with 1 teaspoon butter and serve immediately. (Make sure your vegetables and other side dishes are ready before the fish are.)

Most fish blacken well. When using tuna go to a good market and look for tuna that is bright red. Tuna is best served medium rare so freshness is paramount.

If you want the tuna or other fish cooked more thoroughly put it in a 400 degree oven to finish so that it does not burn. Let the skillet cool down before trying to clean it.

BOUILLABAISSE
Recipe by Chef Loretto "Larry" Pagliara

Bouillabaisse was on the first menu at Charley's Crab on Pine Lake. A traditional seafood stew is great served family style. As Chuck Muer would say, "Roll up your sleeves, quaff a two-bit stein of beer with your Down East Feast and leave the water to the fish."

Yield: 4 servings

2 ounces olive oil
1/4 cup onions, diced
1 teaspoon chopped garlic
1 teaspoon whole fennel
1/2 cup leeks, julienned
Pinch saffron
1 teaspoon salt
Pinch cayenne pepper
8 ounces sherry
5 ounces canned whole tomatoes
Two 1- to 1 1/2-pound lobsters
24 littleneck clams, fresh
32 mussels, fresh
2 pounds fresh fish (salmon, trout or bluefish) cut in 2-inch
    cubes
2 pounds king crab legs
1 cup fresh tomatoes, diced
3/4 cup strained Charley's Chowder (see page 18)
Pinch fresh parsley, chopped
4 pieces garlic toast
4 ounces Cajun Remoulade Sauce (see page 6)

1. In a heavy bottom sauce pan, heat olive oil over low heat until oil becomes bluish in color. Add onions, mix well and cook until golden brown in color.

2. Add garlic and mix well for about 10 seconds.

Chuck Muer knew the extraordinary value of education. He felt strongly about improving its quality for all in the city of Detroit and felt that it was absolutely necessary for the city and for its people, if its workforce was to be enhanced and the renaissance of the city was to be completed. In a very special way he personally supported Saint Martin De Porres High School in Detroit, both financially and through his influence. He saw in this school an unusual success in education, discipline and a healthy dose of good moral values. Because of Chuck's support, many young people were well grounded in this city school and went on to higher pursuits in the universities and colleges of the country. I could always count on his generous help and interest.

–Rev. Msgr. James P. Robinson, S.S.E. Rector, Cathedral of the Most Blessed Sacrament Detroit

*E*arly in my association with Chuck, we traveled to Boston. Between meetings, we were walking through the Marriott on the waterfront. Two sixty-ish Chinese women tourists, who spoke little to no English, were taking each other's picture in front of the large windows overlooking Boston Harbor. Instinctively Chuck new the ladies wanted to have their picture taken together. He rushed over with a big smile, placed the ladies in a scenic spot, snapped the picture, and gave them each a big hug. The ladies chattered and beamed with delight. ... This experience told me what kind of guy we're dealing with here. A strong, goal-oriented businessman who nevertheless always had time for his fellow man. ... I'm proud to say Chuck Muer was my friend. A friendship I'll always treasure.

—Carl W. Freckelton
Grosse Ile, Michigan

3. Add fennel and mix well for about 10 seconds.

4. Add leeks and mix well for 1 minute, increasing heat to high.

5. Stir in saffron and mix well for about 10 seconds.

6. Add salt, tomatoes, cayenne pepper and bring to a boil.

7. Add sherry, mix well and bring to a boil again; cover pot and reduce heat to simmer. Simmer for 5 minutes.

8. Cut lobsters lengthwise and remove stomachs (sac located at nose).

9. In a stainless steel pot, place strained Charley's Chowder, fish, shellfish and Bouillabaisse mixture, cover and cook over high heat for 6 minutes.

10. Carefully transfer all ingredients from the cooking vessel to a decorative serving dish. Pour all of the liquid remaining in the pot over the ingredients in the serving dish. Top with chopped parsley and serve with garlic toast and a dollop of Cajun Remoulade Sauce on the rim of the plate.

PAELLA
Recipe by Chef Loretto "Larry" Pagliara

Paella is a highly disputed preparation, especially in Spain! We use ingredients easily available to us, but the chicken could be substituted with rabbit, the chorizo sausage with Italian sausage, etc. Paella is a great dish for a party and can be done in a large pan designed to serve up to eight people or more. Large paella pans are available at gourmet cookware shops and are made of copper, aluminum and stainless steel, but ceramic-coated cast iron casserole-style pans will serve.

Yield: 4 servings

3 strips raw bacon, diced
1/2 medium Spanish onion, diced
4 large mushrooms, fresh, sliced
1 1/4 cups rice or arborio rice (Italian short grain rice for risotto), uncooked
32 strands saffron
2 ounces pimiento, julienne cut
Pinch cayenne pepper
12 ounces fresh fish, diced in 1-inch chunks (lake trout, salmon, etc.)
4 ounces broccoli spears, fresh
4 ounces green peas, frozen
Four 1-ounce pieces chorizo sausage
4 ounces green pepper, fresh, julienne cut
4 chicken thighs, raw
4 ounces green beans, fresh
12 littleneck clams, fresh (see page 16)
24 mussels, fresh (see page 17)
2 lobsters, fresh, split
20 ounces canned sea clam juice
4 teaspoons parsley, fresh, chopped
2 ounces Casino Butter (see page 12)

Paellas may be made ahead of time up to step eight and then finished at desired time.

*A*rrested by Russian officers May 17, 1982, while speeding on the Autobahn near Berlin, Germany, Betty, Chuck, Judy and I were horrified by the young officers for more than one hour. Finally, with the help of the language barrier, a loaf of bread and bottle of wine, we paid our fine and were released.

–Bill Moore
Port Huron, Michigan

Chuck and Betty were two of my favorite people in the business. But it wasn't just business–they were friends. I loved Betty's independence even though she had such a strong husband. Chuck's enthusiasm was catching! I remember calling Chuck once for a feature story on people's favorite songs. When I asked him, he chuckled and said, "It isn't `Happy Birthday,' I can tell you that!"

–Molly Abraham
Detroit Free Press

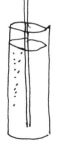

1. Sauté onions and mushrooms with bacon until onions are translucent, then spread on the center of the bottom of a large casserole pan, or pans if you are preparing individual Paella. This protects the rice.

2. Placed uncooked rice over mushroom mixture in the center of the pan.

3. Sprinkle saffron over mixture.

4. Add pimiento and sprinkle cayenne pepper over the top.

5. Arrange fish, broccoli, peas, chorizo and green pepper around rice.

6. Sear the chicken thighs in a pan or on a grill and place along with the vegetables.

7. Cut the lobsters lengthwise, remove the stomachs (the sac at the nose) and place lobster halves in the center of the vegetables.

8. Brush generously with the Casino Butter.

9. Add clam juice, cover and bring to a boil on top of the stove.

10. Add the clams, cover and place in a 450 degree oven for about 10 minutes.

11. Add mussels to pan, cover and cook 5 more minutes in the oven.

12. Remove pan from the oven, be sure cover is still secure, place on top of the stove and boil until all liquid is absorbed by the rice, about 1 minute.

13. Uncover finished Paella and serve immediately.

BRAISED LAMB SHANKS
Recipe by Chef Peter Ashcraft

Braised Lamb Shanks is a very traditional dish in French cooking. At Pal's Charley's Crab in Deerfield Beach, Florida, it is also a very popular and traditional dish. Every Wednesday is lamb shank day, where people line up to eat this succulent dish.

Yield: 4 servings

 4 lamb shanks, weighing 14 to 16 ounces each
4 tablespoons olive oil
1 carrot, roughly diced
1 small onion, roughly diced
1 stalk celery, roughly diced
4 cloves garlic, peeled and crush
4 tablespoons oregano
2 tablespoons kosher salt
1 1/2 tablespoons cracked black pepper
10 ounces chicken broth (fresh or canned)
10 ounces beef broth (fresh or canned)
Arrowroot or corn starch

1. Preheat oven to 325 degrees.

2. Heat heavy bottom sauté pan or dutch oven on top of stove.

3. Season the shanks evenly and prep the vegetables.

4. When pan is very hot add olive oil (oil should be white hot), roll down your sleeves and using a pair of sturdy tongs, carefully place shanks in pan and brown well very evenly on all sides. Stand shanks up, leaning on side of pan to brown bottom side. (You may also want to use some kitchen mitts to avoid splatter burns.)

5. Remove shanks from pan and set aside.

The vegetables strained out of the stock are mushy but exquisite, especially the garlic! More can be added to the recipe. Or julienne some carrots, celery, and onions and steam them.

I knew Chuck Muer my entire life. His mother, Magdalene, had grown up with my grandmother in Anchorville. My father and Chuck made their First Communion together in outfits that Magdalene had to make due to the shortage of white linen during the war. My dad and Chuck graduated from University of Detroit High School together in 1955. When I decided to enter the hospitality industry, I called Chuck for advice and he set up an interview for me with Bob Jones at Charley's Crab in Troy. That interview was the beginning of my restaurant career.

Chuck's passion for food was infectious. I remember him leading a seminar for line cooks and kitchen

managers on how to cook fish "Simply Great." One time, when he and Rocky had been skunked on a fishing trip, they stopped in Sarnia to pick up a sturgeon, which Chuck proceeded to parade through the dining room of the River Crab, telling stories about that ancient fish. When he dined, Chuck made detailed notes about the food and his experience. Whenever Chuck came to one of the units, he made a point of making every employee and guest feel special. He endeared himself so deeply that all who came into contact with him counted Chuck among their friends. After Chuck and Betty disappeared, my father gave me the high school graduation picture that Chuck had signed for him forty years ago. That picture is on my dresser so I think of him when I start my day. It reminds me of the passion and the vision that Chuck had and that I strive for in my life.

–Bill Young
General Manager
Big Fish
Dearborn, Michigan

6. Discard all but about 1 tablespoon of the olive oil, place the pan back on the stove, add vegetable and garlic and sauté until browned.

7. Stir in oregano and allow to cook 1 minute, then add stocks and bring the mixture to a boil, while placing shanks back into the pan with the stock and vegetables.

8. Cover pan with tight fitting lid or aluminum foil and bake in the oven about 3 hours or until the meat is tender, almost falling off the bone.

9. Remove shanks and set aside, covered with saran wrap. Then strain the stock and reduce until flavor is strong. Mix arrowroot or corn starch with a little water and thicken sauce to desired consistency.

10. Ladle sauce over shanks and save some for the potatoes!

SAUTEED SKATE WINGS WITH CAPERS AND BROWN BUTTER
Recipe by Chef Peter Ashcraft

Yield: 4 servings

Four 7 to 8 ounce skate wing fillets
4 tablespoons vegetable oil
1 cup flour
Salt and pepper to season fish
6 tablespoons butter
2 tablespoons fresh lemon juice
2 tablespoons capers

1. Make 3 incisions on back of skin of each fillet.

2. Season skate with salt and pepper, then dredge in flour.

3. Heat a sauté pan, add vegetable oil and place fillets flesh-side down in pan and sauté, adjusting heat to make fillets evenly golden brown. Flip over and brown other side the same way.

4. If fillets are thick, place on a cookie sheet and bake 5 minutes in a 400 degree oven. If not, place in oven 1 minute and prepare butter.

5. To prepare brown butter drain all oil from sauté pan and add butter and return pan to heat. When butter begins to brown, add lemon juice and capers.

6. Remove skate from oven, put on plates, swirl butter around in pan and distribute evenly over each fillet. Serve immediately.

Skate is a North Atlantic species in the ray family. It is highly regarded in Europe and on the East Coast of the United States and Canada as a seafood delicacy.

*M*y thanks to the Muer family! My entry into the restaurant business had an idol and an inspiration–to do it as well as Chuck and his family had done it, and with joy and class. Thanks for that inspiration.

–Ambassador Peter Secchia
Grand Rapids, Michigan

Accompaniments

ENGINE HOUSE NO.5
COLUMBUS

OLGNDORF

Engine House No. 5, Columbus, Ohio . . . century-old fire house in
old-world German Village, where servers slide down the fire pole with
birthday cakes

SIZZLER SPINACH
SCALLOPED POTATOES
BRAISED BLACK AND WHITE BEANS
GINGERED ASIAN VEGETABLES
ROASTED GARLIC RISOTTO
STEWED TOMATOES
BLACK PEPPER SPAETZLE WITH
     BLUE CHEESE
ROOT VEGETABLE GRATINÉE
BRAISED RED CABBAGE
POLENTA

Some years ago, Chuck Muer took a group of his employees to Paris for a "recognition" trip. He kindly asked me to come as a "tour guide translator." I never had so much fun in my entire life. We visited every possible thing in town and none of us slept for more than four hours at a time. ... One afternoon, coming back to the hotel, I saw Betty sprawled on a banquette with her shoes off. She looked at me and said, "I cannot go on," and I replied, "Me neither." Chuck just turned around and said, "Let's go gals," grabbed us by the arms and off we went for a marathon shopping trip. ... His positive demeanor just gave us all the energy to keep grabbing more out of our time together in France. Through the entire journey he exhibited extraordinary kindnesses toward my family (from Paris) and myself. ... I do miss them profoundly.

–Evelyne Mosby
Second Vice President
Private Banking Group
Michigan National Bank
Detroit

SIZZLER SPINACH
Recipe by Chef Loretto "Larry" Pagliara

Chef Larry created this side dish back in the early 1970s for Charley's Crab on Pine Lake and since then it has become one of the more popular dishes through the years.

Yield: 8 servings

1/3 cup vegetable oil
3/4 cup white onion, diced fine
1 clove fresh garlic
3 pounds frozen spinach, defrosted and drained
1 fresh lemon
1 teaspoon salt
Titch ground nutmeg
1 1/2 cups clam broth or clam juice

1. Place the clove of garlic and the vegetable oil in a blender. Purée for 2 minutes.

2. Place the oil mixture into a heated sauté pan. Add onions and sauté for 1 minute.

3. On medium heat add the spinach (make sure it is well drained) and mix well.

4. Add the juice of 1 fresh lemon and mix well.

5. Add the salt and nutmeg, mix well.

6. Add the clam juice, mix well and cover on low heat for 10 minutes.

7. Serve immediately.

SCALLOPED POTATOES
Created by Chef Chuck "Rocky" Rachwitz

This side dish was created for Big Fish in Dearborn, Michigan as a hearty accompaniment to our Simply Great fish.

Yield: 6 servings

6 medium-size whole Idaho potatoes, peeled
3/4 cup white onions, sliced thin julienne cut
2 cloves garlic, chopped fine
1 quart heavy whipping cream
1 1/2 teaspoons salt
1 1/2 tablespoons ground black pepper

1. Preheat oven to 375 degrees.

2. Slice the peeled potatoes very thin (potato chip).

3. Use a 10-inch casserole dish.

4. Mix the potatoes, onions, garlic, salt and pepper together. Place into the casserole dish.

5. Add the heavy cream.

6. Cover with foil and bake at 375 degrees for 1 hour. Remove foil and brown the potatoes for 15 minutes.

7. Serve immediately.

Chuck Muer is a legend, a person who dedicated himself to his vocation professionally and equally so to a dedicated community. He was one of a kind. ... Betty was an admirable partner who made it possible for Chuck to succeed. Her dedication to him, their children, their God and their home was the paramount reason for their happiness and successes. We pray to them in heaven to look down upon us and imbue us with their spirit of giving of ourselves to worthy causes.

–Frank D. Stella
Detroit

More chicken broth may be needed when cooking the beans. When beans are served they should still be a little wet.

The leftover braised beans are excellent served chilled with a little Italian vinaigrette.

*C*huck and I kept in contact over the years since his graduation. It was always a pleasure and inspiration to meet him. No matter how much time had elapsed since our last meeting we could pick up as if we had seen each other yesterday. ... Our conversation would move quickly to his family—especially to the children I had come to know. His pride in them and his affection for them was heart-warming. He was a fine man and a great friend.

–Rev. Joseph O. Schell, S.J.
John Carroll University
Cleveland

BRAISED BLACK AND WHITE BEANS
Recipe by Chef Chuck "Rocky" Rachwitz

Yield: 6 servings

1 cup navy beans
1 cup black beans
1/4 cup White Clam Sauce (see page 11)
1/2 tablespoon salt
1/2 tablespoon pepper
1/4 cup onions, chopped
3 cups chicken broth, canned or fresh
2 tablespoons parsley, chopped
1/4 cup carrots, diced fine

1. In 2 separate sauce pans place 1 ounce of the White Clam Sauce in each. Divide up the onions evenly between the 2 pans and sauté until translucent.

2. Add the navy beans to one pot and the black beans to the other. Evenly split up the salt, pepper and chicken broth and add to each pot.

3. Simmer both pots for approximately 1 1/2 to 2 hours, covered, or until the beans are soft. Set aside.

4. Steam or boil the carrots for 10 minutes or until soft. Add the the carrots and chopped parsley to the white beans (navy beans).

5. Season with salt and pepper.

6. Beans may be mixed or arranged separately for desired presentation.

GINGERED ASIAN VEGETABLES
Recipe by Chef Jim Blake

Yield: 4 servings

24 pea pods (6 per serving)
1 cup carrots, julienne
1/2 cup jicama or daikon radish, julienne
1/4 cup red peppers, julienne
1/2 cup bok choy, chopped
1 1/2 tablespoons garlic, minced
4 tablespoons olive oil
1 tablespoon sesame seeds
2 tablespoons sesame oil
4 tablespoons fresh ginger, grated
2 tablespoons soy sauce

1. Place olive oil in hot sauté pan.

2. Add carrots, red peppers, jicama, pea pods, bok choy and garlic.

3. Sauté 3 minutes.

4. Add sesame oil, ginger and soy sauce.

5. Cook 2 minutes, remove from heat.

6. Top with sesame seeds and divide into four servings.

*O*ne day I stopped at the Big Fish in Dearborn to have Chuck sign some forms. Sitting on a table was a box of the most delightful wooden fish carvings I had ever seen, which were going to be used in the decorating scheme. I asked Chuck where he got them, thinking that they were probably from a big mail-order house "out East." ... He told me that Betty discovered them at Ed Miller's small bait and tackle shop on the St. Clair River up in St. Clair and that Ed carved them. Well, I just had to meet Ed Miller and purchase a couple of his carvings for my collection. After talking to Ed for a while, I soon realized that no matter how successful Chuck and Betty had become, they always had time for and never forgot their old friends.

–Ronald K. Haller
The Haller Insurance
Group
Southfield, Michigan

ROASTED GARLIC RISOTTO
Recipe by Chef Peter Ashcraft

Yield: 4 servings

1 bulb garlic
5 1/2 cups chicken stock or canned chicken broth
1 1/2 cups arborio rice (short grain Italian rice)
2 tablespoons butter
1 tablespoon extra virgin olive oil
1/3 cup finely chopped onion
1/3 cup grated Parmesan cheese

1. Using a sharp knife shave the skin off the top of the garlic bulb, exposing the garlic. Rub with a little olive oil and bake in a 250 degree oven about 45 minutes until garlic is lightly browned and very soft.

2. Allow garlic to cool then extract all the cooked garlic from the bulb. Purée garlic, set aside.

3. Bring chicken stock to a steady simmer in a saucepan.

4. Heat the butter and the olive oil in a heavy duty 4-quart pot over moderate heat. Add the onion and sauté for 1 to 2 minutes, until it becomes translucent, being careful not to brown it.

5. Add the rice and garlic purée, stirring well using a wooden spoon for 1 minute, making sure all the grains are well coated. Begin to add simmered stock, 1/2 cup at a time, stirring frequently. Wait until stock is absorbed before adding next 1/2 cup of stock. Repeat until all stock is absorbed and rice texture is firm but cooked through and very creamy

6. Add the Parmesan cheese and butter. Salt and pepper to taste. Stir well.

Serve immediately.

I fondly remember Chuck and Betty as wonderful patrons of the arts. The following story may illustrate this: When Karen and Mary were still in grade school they asked their parents to hire them to play for a summer party they were having at their home in Grosse Pointe. Chuck said he would if they could work up an hour's program! They went to work on violin and piano and produced a wonderful little repertoire. The entertainment was a success and the girls were launched in musical careers that led them to the Interlochen School of Performing Arts and beyond.

–Sr. Corinne Staub, O.P.
Dayton, Ohio

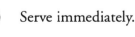

Accompaniments —————— *125*

STEWED TOMATOES
Recipe by Chef Loretto "Larry" Pagliara

Yield: 4 servings

2 pounds Roma tomatoes
1 cup Spanish or Vidalia onions, julienne cut
1/2 cup olive oil
1 tablespoon kosher salt
1/2 teaspoon fresh oregano, chopped
1/2 teaspoon fresh basil, chopped
1 teaspoon garlic, chopped
1 teaspoon pepper, fresh ground

1. Blanch tomatoes in boiling water to soften skin, soak in cold water, peel away skin.

2. Sauté onion and garlic in olive oil until translucent.

3. Add peeled whole tomatoes, fresh basil, oregano, salt and pepper, toss to coat well, simmer 5 minutes.

4. Ready to serve.

We were privileged to share in the lives of Betty and Chuck Muer. Potluck dinners with Chuck asleep by 9:30, the competitive banter of backgammon matches at Charley's Crab, cross-country ski trips with Chuck the chief oyster-shucker, Betty's witty tales of the ongoing family saga and her loyalty to the Monday tennis league are vibrant memories to us. Chuck's exuberance, wit and consuming intensity were balanced by Betty's calm dedication to family, home and personal values. They were genuine, hospitable and warm friends. We miss them.

–Ann and Bob Durand
Port Huron, Michigan

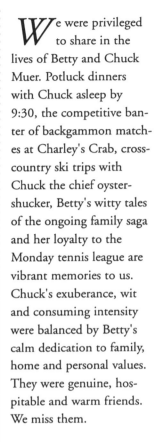

Excellent accompaniment with both meats and fish or as a first course.

*I*n 1963, while working for IBM, Chuck met our father, which was the beginning of a relationship between our family and the C. A. Muer Corporation that still continues. Chuck will always be remembered by us for his creative ability and loyalty.

–Oliver and John Ward
Ward & Ward
Grosse Pointe Woods,
Michigan

BLACK PEPPER SPAETZLE WITH BLUE CHEESE

Yield: 4 to 6 servings

1 cup all purpose flour
1 cup semolina flour
3 eggs
1 1/2 cups milk
1 tablespoon kosher salt
1 tablespoon course ground black pepper
1/2 cup blue cheese, crumbled
1 Spanish onion, julienne
2 tablespoons butter
2 tablespoons parsley, fresh, chopped

1. Place dry ingredients in mixing bowl, add eggs and milk, mix well, until smooth (spaetzle batter).

2. Bring a large pot of salted water to a boil.

3. Place a colander over pot, place spaetzle batter in colander and push through with rubber spatula.

4. Remove spaetzle from boiling water when it floats to the top. Cool under cold water, add a little vegetable oil to prevent sticking.

5. In a sauté pan add butter and melt.

6. Add onion and sauté over medium heat. Cook until the onions start to caramelize.

7. Add spaetzle and cook until they brown, stirring occasionally.

8. Add blue cheese and toss well. Do not melt the blue cheese all the way.

To Serve: Place on 4 to 6 individual plates and serve immediately.

ROOT VEGETABLE GRATINÉE
Recipe created by Chef Jim Blake

Yield: 6 servings

1 cup heavy cream
1 medium-size baking potato
1 parsnip
1 sweet potato
1 small celery root (also called celeriac)
1/3 cup chives, fresh, sliced
3/4 cup Parmesan cheese, preferably fresh Reggiano Parmesan
1 teaspoon salt
1/2 teaspoon white pepper
Pinch of nutmeg
1 teaspoon butter, softened

1. Peel vegetables and julienne cut 1/8-inch thick.

2. In small stainless steel bowl, combine the heavy cream, salt, pepper and nutmeg. In another bowl, combine the vegetables, tossing them to evenly distribute.

3. Generously butter a baking or casserole dish. Layer half of the vegetable mixture in the pan, slightly pressing them into an even layer. Pour half of the cream mixture over the vegetables.

4. Sprinkle with chives and 1/2 cup Parmesan cheese.

5. Layer with remaining vegetables. Pour remaining cream over the vegetables and sprinkle with 1/4 cup Parmesan cheese.

6. Cover with foil and bake in a preheated 350 degree oven for 30 minutes; uncover and continue to bake for another 30 minutes until bubbly and nicely browned. Do not overbake or allow the cream to be completely absorbed. Dish should be creamy.

The faculty, staff, and students of The Culinary Institute of America had the great pleasure of having Chuck Muer address the graduating class on June 7, 1991, as commencement speaker. In his very impassioned commencement speech, Chuck shared his life's philosophies and his operating principles with our graduates. ... The Institute not only lost an industry leader and staunch supporter, but a person committed to exemplary values. We shall all miss him.

–Ferdinand E. Metz
President, The Culinary
Institute of America
Hyde Park, New York

Vegetables may be prepared in advance and stored in water in the refrigerator.

Chuck Muer was not only one of the finest restaurateurs to ever grace the Midwest, his restaurants led across the country. But he was a Michigan person all the way. His entrepreneurial abilities were exceptional. His innovative knowledge of the food business was outstanding and almost unique. It was a pleasure for me to have known him and to have learned at his hand. He gave to the entire Michigan community so very generously all his life. He was a wonderful friend, an outstanding business man and a most delightful restaurateur.

–R. D. Musser
Chairman, Grand Hotel
Mackinac Island,
Michigan

Best served with pork, veal or game.

BRAISED RED CABBAGE
Recipe by Chef Chuck "Rocky" Rachwitz

Yield: 6 to 8 servings

1 head cabbage sliced 1/4 inch by 2 inches
1 red onion, julienne cut
1 cup dry red wine
1 teaspoon ground cloves
1 cup chicken broth
2 tablespoons corn starch
2 tablespoons cold water
1 1/2 teaspoons kosher salt
1 teaspoon fresh ground pepper
1 teaspoon chopped garlic

1. Place sliced cabbage, onions, cloves, garlic and red wine in stainless steel bowl and mix together well.

2. Cover and refrigerate, allow to marinate overnight.

3. In a sauté pan, cook cabbage mixture on medium heat until cabbage is tender.

4. Add chicken stock and bring to a soft boil.

5. In a separate bowl mix together corn starch, water.

6. Add to cabbage stirring until sauce has formed.

7. Add salt and pepper to taste.

POLENTA
Recipe by Chef Chuck "Rocky" Rachwitz

Yield: 8 servings

6 cups water
2 2/3 cups yellow cornmeal
8 tablespoons fresh grated parmesan
2 tablespoons butter
To taste kosher salt and cracked black pepper

1. In a heavy duty pot bring water to a boil.

2. Add salt and pepper.

3. Slowly add cornmeal in a steady stream.

4. Reduce heat to a simmer and continue to stir, breaking up lumps. Continue stirring on and off for about 20 minutes, until Polenta stops sticking to the sides of pan.

5. Add butter and Parmesan and stir until smooth. Check seasonings.

6. Polenta can be served immediately or spread into a baking pan, allowed to cool, and cut into squares or other shapes and grilled, sautéed, or fried.

Fresh cut corn cut off the cob makes an excellent garnish to be stirred in when adding butter and Parmesan.

Try a square of polenta, dredged in corn meal or cracker meal and sautéed until very crispy, bake in oven and top with Chef Larry's Provençal Sauce *(see page 10)*.

*C*huck Muer had more good ideas on promoting and marketing the food and beverage industry than all the books that were ever written on the subject. His energy and enthusiasm were contagious and he influenced and energized everyone who was fortunate enough to have been associated with him. He was a good friend and one who gave of himself no matter what the cause. Detroiters were lucky to have him in their community.

–Anthony M. Franco
Chairman, Anthony M.
Franco Inc.
Detroit

Desserts

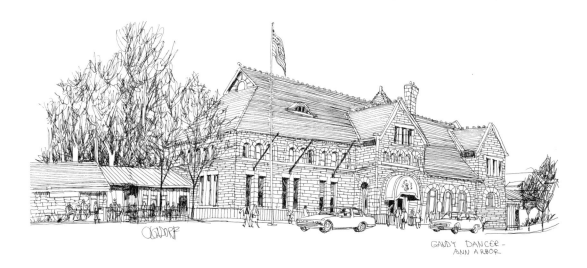

Gandy Dancer, *Ann Arbor, Michigan . . . magnificent 1886 depot with glass-walled trackside room and other romantic dining "on the line"*

FRESH FRUIT GAZPACHO
WHITE CHOCOLATE CHEESECAKE
CHOCOLATE DECADENCE
SHARK FIN PIE
STRAWBERRY NAPOLEON
BUTTERCREAM FROSTING
CHOCOLATE SAUCE
CARAMEL SAUCE
YELLOW SPONGE CAKE
WHITE CHOCOLATE MOUSSE
BLACKBERRY PIE
PIE CRUST
THE GREAT WALL
CARROT CAKE
CREAM CHEESE FROSTING
CARAMEL MACADAMIA NUT TORTE

Of all the wonderful memories I have of Chuck Muer, my favorite is the "Kite Flight Crew." It was a beautiful day, sunny and warm, with a cool breeze blowing in off the Detroit River. Fifty or sixty Muer employees met on the rooftop parking area of Cobo Hall to fly kites. It was a morning full of laughter and camaraderie. I was always in awe of both the incredible rapport Chuck had with his employees and the wonderful creativity he had for finding new and different ways to have fun.

–Robert Bossio
Executive Chef
Huron River Hunting and
Fishing Club
Farmington, Michigan

They would drive me crazy. There was not one ounce of "curmudgeon" in either one of them. How could people stand them?

–Ed Draves
Bad Axe, Michigan

FRESH FRUIT GAZPACHO
Recipe by Chef Jim Blake

This dessert is great for a hot summer picnic or gettogether. Always refreshing and simple to prepare!

Yield: 8 servings

1 star fruit (carambola), sliced
4 kiwi fruits, peeled and sliced
1 quart fresh strawberries, washed, sliced
2 pints raspberries, washed
2 pints blueberries, washed
1 cup sugar

1. Toss each fruit in separate bowls with 1/4 cup of sugar. Place in refrigerator and allow to marinate at least 4 hours.

2. In a clear glass bowl layer the fruits as follows: strawberries on the bottom, then kiwi, then blueberries and raspberries on top. Garnish with the sliced star fruit.

Desserts ———————————— 135

WHITE CHOCOLATE CHEESECAKE
Recipe by Pastry Chef Carmen Vilican

Yield: one 9" cake
8 servings

Crust:
1 cup chocolate wafer crumbs
1/4 cup butter, melted

Filling:
2 pounds cream cheese, at room temperature
1 cup sugar
4 eggs
2 egg yolks (in addition to 4 eggs)
12 ounces white chocolate, chopped, melted
1 tablespoon vanilla extract
1/3 cup butter, very soft
1/2 cup heavy cream
2 tablespoons cornstarch

1. Preheat oven to 300 degrees.

2. Combine the wafer crumbs and melted butter in a bowl
    and mix together well.

3. In a 9"x 3" springform pan, press with your hands the
    crumbs firmly and evenly on the bottom of the pan.
    Set aside.

4. In a bowl melt the chopped white chocolate over hot,
    not boiling, water. Whip with a whisk until chocolate is
    smooth. Set aside to cool; cover chocolate to keep luke
    warm.

5. With a mixer, beat together the cream cheese and sugar
    until smooth, about 10 minutes. Scrape the
    bowl well with a rubber spatula after 5
    minutes.

Bain-Marie was originally a term used in alchemy. It was then referred to as bain de marie (Mary's Bath) after Moses's sister, who was an alchemist. It is a utensil used in cooking patés and pastry without burning them, or for cooking dishes very slowly.

*M*y wife, Nina, and I remember Betty ... as a beautiful person, in appearance and in nature, as outgoing, friendly and charming, both as a little girl and as an adult. ... I could see Chuck's genius, his ability to plan and carry out his plans. ... He could see the bigger picture and yet implement the necessary small, important details that are essential to the public food service. ...

6. On low speed add the eggs and egg yolks one at a time. Scrape down the mixture after each egg to ensure the batter is well mixed.

7. Slowly add the vanilla, white chocolate, and very soft butter. Scrape down batter and beat on low for 2 minutes.

8. In a cup mix together the cornstarch and heavy cream. Add it to the cheesecake batter slowly. Scrape down batter.

9. Pour the batter into the prepared springform pan. Shake pan carefully to get rid of any air bubbles in the batter.

10. Place the springform pan on a sheet tray and add warm water to fill sheet pan half full (Bain-Marie).

11. Place sheet tray into the preheated 300 degree oven for 1 1/2 hours, or until the cheesecake springs back in the middle. If needed, add more water to the sheet tray.

12. Cool the cheesecake at least 2 hours before serving.

Desserts

CHOCOLATE DECADENCE
Recipe by Pastry Chef Carmen Vilican

The devil made us do this dessert! It is sinfully delicious and is a favorite among the most serious of chocolate devotees!

Yield: one 9" cake
10 servings

1 pound semi-sweet chocolate, chopped
5 ounces butter
5 eggs, room temperature
1 tablespoon sugar
1 tablespoon all purpose flour
1 cup Chocolate Sauce (see page 143)
1 cup whipped cream

1. Combine the chocolate and butter in a bowl and melt over hot water, not boiling water. Set aside.

2. Combine eggs and sugar in a bowl and whisk over hot water until the sugar is dissolved.

3. With a beater whip the eggs until tripled in volume (5 to 10 minutes).

4. Gently fold with a rubber spatula the whipped eggs and flour together.

5. Gently fold the melted chocolate into the whipped eggs.

6. Pour batter into a 9-inch cake pan and bake in a preheated 400 degree oven for 18 minutes, cool.

7. Remove cooled cake from pan and drizzle the chocolate sauce evenly over the cake. Serve with a dollop of freshly whipped cream.

I was only able to work with Chuck for four months before he and Betty's tragic disappearance. The one thing that stays in my mind, to this day, is how open Chuck was to new ideas. He had been running the company for 28 years before I came on board as the Corporate Executive Chef. It really impacted upon me because he and I shared the same intense pursuit of new ideas, the same quality standards and the same love of seafood. He was always looking for new species of fish to try, new concepts for future restaurants, always pushing the creative envelope. It was so refreshing to start a new job and to have the exposure to a man like Chuck Muer. He was a man of obvious self-confidence to be able to encourage my ideas and recipes instead of "pigeon holing" me into a traditional Corporate Chef's role. The continuing success of C. A. Muer restaurants is a testament to a Giant among men.

–Jim Blake
Corporate Executive Chef
C. A. Muer Corporation

A number of years ago Chuck was chairman of the service industry of the United Way Fund Drive and "volunteered" me to handle the restaurant division. We proceeded to reach our goal and while celebrating at the Pontch I mentioned how much I enjoyed the Charley's Chowder. The next thing I knew here comes Chuck with a gallon jug of the wonderful stuff for me to take home. That kind of gesture was quite typical of him.

–Thomas Pavloff
VP Sales-Food Service
Cadillac Coffee Company
Detroit

SHARK FIN PIE
Recipe by Chef Chuck "Rocky" Rachwitz

Yield: one 9" pie
8 servings

1 gallon chocolate swirl or coffee ice cream
2 cups hot fudge sauce, preferably Sanders Hot Fudge
1 cup chocolate wafer crumbs
1 cup whipping cream
1/2 cup sugar
1 cup pecan pieces, toasted

1. Soften the ice cream at room temperature for 15 minutes or until soft and pliable.

2. Press ice cream into a 9-inch pie pan mounding ice cream high in the center.

3. Place ice cream pie in the freezer for at least 1 hour.

4. Remove pie from the freezer and dip the bottom of the pan in hot water and remove ice cream pie from pan.

5. Cut the pie into 8 equal sections and coat each slice generously with the chocolate wafer crumbs. Return each slice to the freezer when finished coating.

6. Whip the cream with a beater, slowly adding sugar. Do not overwhip.

7. Place a 2-ounce ladle of heated hot fudge on 8 plates. Place a slice of pie standing upright on each, top with whipped cream and sprinkle with the toasted pecans.

STRAWBERRY NAPOLEON
Recipe by Chef Dorothy Lewis

Yield: 4 servings

2 cups half & half
4 egg yolks
5 ounces sugar
8 tablespoons cornstarch
6 ounces butter, at room temperature
1 teaspoon vanilla extract
3 quarts strawberries, fresh
1/2 cup sugar
2 cups water
1 sheet puff pastry cut into 4 triangles
1/4 cup powdered sugar, for garnish

1. Rinse, drain and slice in halves 2 quarts of strawberries. Set aside.

2. Cut the puff pastry into 4 large rectangles (4" x 10"). Bake puff pastry triangles in a preheated 325 degree oven for 15 minutes or until golden brown. When cooled slice each rectangle in halves to make 4 tops and 4 bottoms.

3. Clean and cut stems off 1 quart of strawberries. Place in a pot with 1 cup of water and 1/2 cup of sugar. Bring to a boil, remove from heat and strain strawberries through a china cap to remove the pulp. In a bowl measure 2 tablespoons cornstarch and mix with 1 1/2 cups water. Add slowly to the strained strawberries. Place on medium heat and cook until thickened. Set aside to cool.

4. Bring the half & half to a quick boil on high heat. Remove the half & half immediately upon boiling. Set aside. Whip by hand with a whisk the 5 ounces of sugar, 6 tablespoons cornstarch and the 4 egg yolks for 5 minutes or until sugar dissolves and mixture turns white. Add the half & half SLOWLY to the egg yolk mixture.

*A*s Betty Muer's sister, writing a short tribute to her is not an easy task. She was certainly a unique person, full of fun, life and love. To summarize, she was a loving, generous sister, a devoted and loyal wife, a mother who gave unconditional love to her children, and a wonderful friend. I miss her more than words can say. I write a tribute to Chuck for his great business acumen and creative mind. My husband and I were always proud to go to one of his fine restaurants offering creative dishes and excellent service. No tribute can be complete concerning the legacy Chuck and Betty have left their children without recognition of our father, Kent Zimmerman, who was instrumental in helping Chuck get started and for giving many years of support and guidance.

—Bonnie Zimmerman Wachter
Grosse Pointe Farms
Michigan

In 1989 I created a retail shop called the Concourse Collection at the Grand Concourse. Sales of clothing and train-related items were good but had not reached my projections. During a visit to Pittsburgh, Chuck and I discussed the shop and he said, "Rick, your problem is that you are not a retail guy, you are an old saloon-keeper like me." He offered to have Betty shop for merchandise for us, then redo the shop in a way that sales would grow. Shortly thereafter, the Wooden Whistle shop was born. In addition to the signature train whistles that Betty found, many unique gifts were added. Years later, the caring and creativity of Chuck and Betty are alive and well in Pittsburgh. Thank you, Chuck, for the vision and wisdom that continues today.

–Rick McMaster
Grand Concourse
Pittsburgh

Pour the mixture back into pot and return to stove on medium heat. Cook mixture to a boil by STIRRING CONSTANTLY with a wooden spoon. When mixture boils, cook for 3 minutes longer and remove from heat. Pour the hot mixture into a mixing bowl and whip until cool, then slowly add the butter and vanilla.

5. Spoon the pastry cream generously on the bottom of each puff pastry triangle, then generously layer the uncooked sliced strawberries over the pastry creme. Spoon another layer of pastry creme over the strawberries and cover with the puff pastry tops.

6. Set the pastries on 4 dessert plates and pour the strawberry sauce over the pastries. Garnish with extra strawberry slices and dust each Napoleon with powdered sugar.

BUTTERCREAM FROSTING
Recipe by Chef Carmen Vilican

Yield: one 9" torte

1 1/2 pounds unsalted butter, at room temperature
3/4 cup egg whites
2 1/2 cups confectioners (powdered) sugar
2 teaspoons vanilla extract
1 teaspoon almond extract

1. Cream butter in a mixer with a whip on medium speed until very light and fluffy.

2. In a separate bowl whip the egg whites on medium speed until stiff, be careful to not overwhip. On low speed slowly add the powdered sugar 1/2 cup at a time. Whip until the sugar is incorporated.

3. Turn mixer on medium and slowly add the whipped butter to the egg whites. Whip until smooth, about 5 minutes.

4. Add the vanilla and almond extract.

5. Set aside at room temperature until needed.

*C*huck was a teacher, one who always had a great sense of the direction you should head. He helped bring out that entrepreneurial and restaurateur spirit in many of us. Every time we spoke, his words would invoke thought and action. He touched many of his employees in much the same way. A little bit of Chuck lives in us all, his beliefs and values; that's where the real joy in working in his restaurants comes out.

–Tony G. Gee
Big Fish • Too
Madison Heights,
Michigan

*C*huck Muer always strove for excellence and perfection in his life and business. My acquaintance with him grew out of his determination to select the best house wines for his restaurants, those

that would bear his name. Most restaurant proprietors call a wholesaler or distributor or a favorite winery and give them the task of making the choice. But not Chuck Muer. Each year he assembled a group comprised of members of his staff and those of us professionally involved in wine judging and wine education. With the wine bottles concealed, we would taste a variety of wines, not knowing the producer or the price. Then we would discuss the merits of the wine we liked best, all with a view to the consumer, in this case the restaurant patron. When a consensus was achieved, that red and white wine bore the Muer Selection label. When next you select a Muer red or white wine, know that this great and humble man is looking down from on high and toasting to your good health.

–Joseph J. Schagrin
President, International
Director
Tasters Guild
Ft. Lauderdale, Florida

CHOCOLATE SAUCE
Recipe by Chef Carmen Vilican

Yield: 1 cup

10 ounces semisweet chocolate, chopped
3/4 cup heavy cream

1. Place cream in medium-size saucepan and slowly bring to a boil.

2. Remove pan from heat.

3. Pour over chocolate, let stand for 5 minutes.

4. Mix until smooth.

CARAMEL SAUCE
Recipe by Chef Carmen Vilican

Yield: 1 cup

1 cup sugar
1/4 cup water
1/2 cup heavy cream

1. Place sugar and water in a heavy bottom saucepan and stir until sugar is dissolved.

2. Cook over high heat until sugar is golden brown.

3. Slowly add heavy cream, stirring constantly.

4. Bring mixture back to a boil and boil for 3 minutes.

Desserts

143

YELLOW SPONGE CAKE
Recipe by Chef Carmen Vilican

Yield: one 9" cake

6 eggs
1 cup sugar
1 cup flour, sifted
1/2 cup vegetable oil
1 1/2 teaspoons vanilla

1. Combine eggs and sugar in mixing bowl, warm over hot water until sugar is dissolved.

2. Whip with a mixer until light and fluffy and four times the original volume.

3. Fold in 1/2 cup flour to the eggs then add 1/4 cup of the oil and the vanilla.

4. Fold in the remaining flour and oil.

5. Pour the batter into a buttered 9"x 3" cake pan and bake at 325 degrees for about 35 minutes or until a toothpick inserted in the center comes out clean.

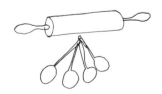

I would like to pay a tribute to Chuck Muer for teaching us to have a "sense of generosity." He used his Grandfather Joe as an example. He would always have candy for the children at the end of their meal. That sense of generosity stuck with Chuck and he passed it on to us and many others in our company. Some examples are the bluefish pate, which is served complimentary before every meal, and the chocolate-dipped fruit after dinner. His generosity included the employees of our corporation. Through profit sharing, stock options, and the ABC bonus package, there isn't a more generous plan of compensation in the industry. Chuck always took care of his guests and employees through his wonderful sense of generosity.

–John Spoto
General Manager
Charley's Crab Palm Beach
Palm Beach, Florida

Desserts

About five years ago, twenty or so 1955 graduates of the University of Detroit High School got together for a social gathering to play cards. Just before we started to play, Chuck Muer asked if he could say a few words to us. He talked about U. of D.H.S. and the wonderful things that were happening there. He advised all of us to go to the school and see the improvements to the school and the educational system. He also talked about his work with city of Detroit officials, business people and educators in trying to develop an education system to help the less fortunate families and children of Detroit. Chuck Muer loved to play cards, but on that night we never did. We listened in awe to his dedication to education for the people of Detroit.

–Tom Vesnaugh
Redford Township,
Michigan

WHITE CHOCOLATE MOUSSE
Recipe by Chef Carmen Vilican

Yields: 3 cups
4 servings

6 ounces white chocolate, chopped
2 tablespoons butter
2 egg whites
1 1/2 cups heavy cream (whipping)
2 tablespoons sugar

1. Combine chocolate and butter in the top of a double boiler, over hot, not boiling, water.

2. While chocolate is melting whip the heavy cream to soft peaks.

3. Whip egg whites in a clean bowl to stiff peaks while slowly adding the sugar.

4. Remove the chocolate from the heat and gently fold in the whipped egg whites.

5. Gently fold in the whipped cream, just until combined.

6. Cover and refrigerate at least 1 hour before serving.

Desserts

BLACKBERRY PIE
Recipe by Chef Jim Blake

Yield: one 9" pie
serves 8

5 cups blackberries, fresh
1 cup granulated sugar
3 tablespoons corn starch
1 teaspoon lemon juice, freshly squeezed
1/4 teaspoon cinnamon
Pie Crust (see page 147)

1. Prepare Pie Crust.

2. Divide pie crust in half, place half of the dough on a floured table, roll to a 12 inch circle.

3. Place crust in a buttered 9-inch pie pan.

4. Combine all other ingredients and place in the pie shell you just prepared.

5. Roll out remaining dough to 1/4-inch thick and cut into 1/2-inch wide strips.

6. Place strips in lattice on top of the pie, trim extra crust around edge of pie pan.

7. Brush top of pie with milk and bake in a 375 degree pre-heated oven for 40 to 50 minutes.

For all his successes, [Chuck] never dwelled upon himself, upon his achievements or upon his financial success. Chuck would sit patiently and listen while others would expound. ...

A small example of this occurred at a John Carroll classmate assemblage in Chicago in early 1991. My wife mentioned to a group of classmates and their wives that she and I were going to return to the St. Clair Inn for a second honeymoon on our wedding anniversary in October. Naturally, I was more than a little embarrassed, because Chuck's premier restaurant and motel is just down the road from the St. Clair Inn. ... Betty graciously commented on how near the freighters came to the St. Clair Inn and what a romantic, spectacular sight it was from the rooms at night. Many months later when my wife and I checked into our room at the St. Clair Inn, we were greeted by an iced bottle of Chuck's excellent wine, two wine glasses, flowers and a lovely note of congratulations. As always,

Chuck had been listening to everything that others had been saying at the gathering of classmates many months previous. ... Chuck and Betty will be greatly missed by all who knew them. They will certainly be missed by me for as long as I live.

–William P. Marks
White Pigeon, Michigan

PIE CRUST

Yield: one 9" pie
double crust

2 cups flour
1/2 teaspoon salt
2 teaspoons sugar
2/3 cup vegetable shortening (NOT oil)
5 tablespoons cold water

1. Combine flour, salt, and sugar in a bowl.

2. Mix until it resembles course meal.

3. Add cold water and mix by hand just until it forms a ball.

4. Cover with plastic wrap and refrigerate at least 30 minutes.

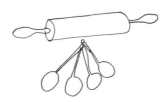

THE GREAT WALL
Recipe by Chef Jim Blake

Yield: 4 servings

Almond Meringue
White Chocolate Mousse
Chocolate Sauce (see page 143)
Caramel Sauce (see page 143)

STEP 1—ALMOND MERINGUE

1 pound of almonds, ground or finely chopped
1 1/4 cups granulated sugar
4 egg whites
1/2 tablespoon almond extract

1. Line cookie sheet (with sides) with parchment paper; butter and flour parchment paper.

2. Beat egg whites to soft peaks. Add the sugar a little at a time.

3. Fold in the almond extract and the almonds.

4. Spread evenly on the lined cookie sheet.

5. Bake at 300 degrees until golden brown.

6. Remove from the oven and deeply score several sections each measuring 2 1/2" x 3" (at least 16 pieces needed to create boxes, four pieces per box). Then return to the oven until crisp. Cool. Remove from paper. Break into rectangles using pre-scored (cuts) lines.

STEP TWO—WHITE CHOCOLATE MOUSSE

1 pound white chocolate, finally chopped
1 cup whole milk
1 quart whipping cream
3 1/2 sheets gelatin (this is bakers gelatin and may be purchased at most grocery stores)
1/2 pound white chocolate, cut into chips

C huck Muer was an unusual man, and when you got to know him, you realized what a tremendous personality he was. The first time I met him was in Pittsburgh for the opening of the Grand Concourse Restaurant. My company started supplying the Grand Concourse with seafood products, and from this initial meeting we started to supply many of his restaurants in the Midwest and in Florida. ... I looked forward to talking to him about our businesses, family, personal activities, and many facets of life. Frequently, when he was in Pittsburgh, my wife and I had dinner with

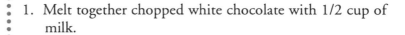

him. The time spent during these evenings was always warm and memorable, and transcended the typical business relationship.

He was a great and talented man with a lust for life, work, play, and above all, family. He and Betty ... were an example to all of us of the true meaning of the word *love*. I still cherish my relationship with Chuck Muer, and consider my life enriched by the friendship we maintained.

–Bernard Benkovitz
Nordic Fisheries Inc.
Pittsburgh

1. Melt together chopped white chocolate with 1/2 cup of milk.

2. Soak gelatin sheets in the other 1/2 cup of milk. Dissolve over heat.

3. Beat whipping cream to soft peaks and fold this into the melted chocolate.

4. Fold in gelatin and the white chocolate chips.

5. Cool, hold for later use.

STEP 3—ASSEMBLY

8 3" rectangle walls
8 2 1/2 square walls
16 ounces white chocolate mousse
6 ounces Chocolate Sauce (see page 143)
6 ounces Caramel Sauce (see page 143)

1. Place 1 ounce white chocolate mousse on a plate, per serving.

2. Stick walls into mousse and lean against each other, use 2-3" rectangular walls and 2-2 1/2" square walls per box.

3. Fill each box with 3 ounces white chocolate mousse.

4. Drizzle into each open box, on top of the chocolate mousse, 1 1/2 ounce chocolate and 1 1/2 ounce caramel sauce. Use back and forth motion, free form.

5. Serve immediately.

CARROT CAKE
Recipe by Chef Carmen Vilican

Yield: One 9" cake
8 servings

3 eggs
1 cup sugar
1 cup vegetable oil
1 1/2 cups flour
1 1/4 teaspoons cinnamon
1 teaspoon baking powder
1 1/4 teaspoons baking soda
1/2 teaspoon salt
2 cups carrots, shredded
1 cup walnuts, chopped
Cream Cheese Frosting (see page 151)

1. Preheat oven to 325 degrees.

2. Place eggs in a mixing bowl and while beating eggs, slowly add sugar and then oil.

3. Sift together flour, cinnamon, baking powder, baking soda, and salt.

4. Add carrots, all dry ingredients, and walnuts to egg mixture and beat until combined.

5. Pour batter into a greased 9-inch pan and bake for 35 minutes or until center of cake springs back when touched.

6. Cool cake completely.

7. Cut cake into three even layers.

8. Fill each layer and frost the sides and top with the Cream Cheese Frosting.

*A*t a recent reunion, we instituted a "man of the year" award to be given to that individual whose actions and efforts went above and beyond. The choice of Chuck Muer as our first recipient was an easy one--not because of his success as a restaurateur and entrepreneur, but because of the extraordinary generosity he exhibited to John Carroll University, to our class [of '59] and to individuals like Dick Tobin (Betty Muer played a big role in that generosity). When we put out the call for a support dinner to be held in Chicago for Marty Dempsey, the first response I got was from Chuck. After expressing his concern, he stated simply, "Betty and I will be there." That, to me, summed up the Muers. When there was a crisis, Betty and Chuck were there! This world is a better place for the time they spent with us. Our thoughts and prayers are with their family and loved ones.

–Gerald F. Burke
Arlington Heights, Illinois

*I*n the game of life, if the winners are decided by the number of friends they have accumulated, Chuck and Betty would surely be declared the winners. No matter what you did for them, they always managed to do more for you.

–Mike Peacock
Dynamic Products Inc.
Livonia, Michigan

CREAM CHEESE FROSTING

Yield: 3 cups fill and frost one 9 inch cake

16 ounces cream cheese, room temperature
1/2 cup butter, room temperature
3/4 cup powdered sugar
1 teaspoon vanilla
1 teaspoon orange zest, grated

Combine all ingredients in mixing bowl and beat until light and fluffy.

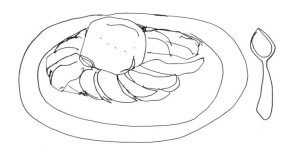

CARAMEL MACADAMIA NUT TORTE
Recipe by Chef Carmen Vilican

Yields: one 9" cake
10 servings

One 9-inch yellow sponge cake (see page 144)
1 quart heavy cream
1/2 cup powdered sugar
2 cups macadamia nuts, chopped
1 1/2 cups Caramel Sauce (see page 143)
4 cups Buttercream Frosting(see page 142)
1/2 cup rum

1. Prepare sponge cake and place on waxed cake circle or serving plate, cut into 3 even layers. Set cake aside.

2. Whip heavy cream with powdered sugar until stiff, fold in macadamia nuts.

3. Spread 1/4 cup Caramel Sauce on bottom layer of cake, then spread with one half of the whipped cream.

4. Set second cake layer on top and repeat the caramel and whipped cream layering.

5. Set third cake layer on top and chill.

6. Prepare Buttercream Frosting and add remaining 1 cup of Caramel Sauce and rum.

7. Frost cake with flavored Buttercream.

*C*huck Muer's life was packed with fun, action and excitement. He could eat an enormous amount of food and burn it all off with his incredible energy. He was a genial host and a generous employer, who made a tremendous impact on anyone he ever met.

–Milos Cihelka, CMC
Bloomfield Hills,
Michigan

—Leo Beil
President
C.A. Muer Corporation

I was transferred in the fall of 1958 by the Sheraton Corporation from the William Penn Hotel in Pittsburgh to the Sheraton Cadillac in Detroit. In Early 1963 I began to realize that I.B.M. was the future in office systems. I approached my general manager who suggested that I contact I.B.M. and they sent in a sales representative by the name of Chuck Muer. We worked about a year putting the system together and when it was time to make the presentation, the general manager was conveniently out of town and we were turned over to his assistant who out-of-hand rejected the proposal. Needless to say, Chuck and I were both dejected. I parted way thinking what a great guy Chuck was but probably would never see him again.

Six months later Chuck asked my help to open the new hotel being built down at the river's edge, later to be called the "Hotel Pontchartrain". At first I rejected the offer because not only did I have 13 years with Sheraton, I also had six kids and a wife. I really couldn't take too many chances with a new hotel and, if jobless down the road, be able to feed all those mouths. After a family consultation I decided to go with Chuck, and as the saying goes, "Here I am today!".

As it turned out, thank God I did. Over the next thirty years Chuck (who I affectionately called "Charlie Brown") and I became great friends. In fact he became the "brother" I never had. We worked hard, we played hard (sometimes too hard), and before we knew it we were running a seventy-five-million dollar company with thirty-one restaurants in nine states.

Winston Churchill once said, "A friend is one who walks in when others walk out." To me that was Chuck Muer. In good times and in bad, he was always there for his friends. And for a man that had literally hundreds of friends, that was no easy task.

There was a time not too many years ago when I was going in for surgery and wasn't sure I'd be coming back to talk about it. When Chuck walked into my hospital room I decided it was time to let him know a few things I'd been keeping to myself. Not all favorable mind you. Well, to make a long story short, the surgery was successful, and my thoughts quickly switched from life or death to, gee I wonder if I still have a job after all I shared with Chuck. When I called him to apologize for my cantankerous remarks he stopped me and said, "Leo, you don't have to explain anything. We've come along way together and we have a lot longer journey ahead. How soon can you get back to work?" We never discussed it again.

When I came to the realization that Chuck had taken his final journey, I spent the evening in my wine cellar with a large glass of cabernet and one of the Havana cigars he had given me for Christmas. I reminisced about all the wonderful memories we shared and how different my life would have been had I not believed in Chuck, and his dream some twenty-seven years earlier. And even though I've felt a tremendous loss, I'll take with me always the happiness and strengths that my "brother" Chuck gave me.

When first we met, so long ago,
  Your smile was mellow and eyes all aglow.
With blond curly hair, no lines on your face,
  Immense vim and vigor and yet full of grace.

A very young man with a family to feed,
  You knew exactly what you would need.
Long hours the standard but that was just fine,
  Your dreams were filled of food and wine.

Detroit to Aspen and Troy to Palm Beach,
  Family and "Friends" you continued to teach.
With Larry and Leo entrenched by your side,
  Your empire grew on a foundation of pride.

Young people would come to learn your technique,
  Then off they would go, their own fortune to seek.
You knew their plan right from the start,
  Always willing to help when time came to part.

You opened your arms to welcome us in,
  And stayed by our side through thick and thin.
When things did not meet your own expectation,
  You'd gather us in for a quick explanation.

Through troubled times you were always there,
  To lend an ear and counsel with care.
In times of joy and in times of grief,
  You helped us hold fast to our own belief.

Each passing year we would reminisce,
  Of the Pontch, the people and things we'd missed.
Your love for family was most important,
  For Betty, Chuck, Mari & Karen, for Susan, Julie, Matt & Kent.

We can search and search our whole life through,
  And never find a greater friend than you.
Over the years our friendship grew,
  To a deep devotion known only by a few.

We now face the future without your insight,
  Difficult decisions but we'll NOT take flight.
You taught us so much throughout the years,
  We draw on that knowledge to calm our fears.

GO
DEAREST
FRIEND

by Donna Bauer

Your office is there, the round table awaits,
  For those meetings you hosted with such a gait.
We enter that space and expect to see,
  Your braces, bow tie and chuckles of glee.

You sailed and skied and swam with the porpoise,
  You hunted for duck and searched for a tortoise.
Your thirst for life is what made you soar,
  You did so much, yet still wanted more.

Your life was filled with toil and fun,
  Even off to Spain with the bulls you did run.
To help the impoverished, to educate our young,
  So much to do and you had just begun.

You've left a great legacy which fills us with pride,
  We will endure as if you're by our side.
We may stagger and fumble as we carry on,
  Your impassioned creed still shines like the sun.

Your eyes are now closed and your laughter has waned,
  For love of your family you would do it again.
Your mission on earth is finally complete,
  The Lord has beckoned, His voice oh so sweet.

There is so much more for me to say,
  As our lives intermingled from day to day.
Those thirty years flew by in a snap,
  Just one storm ... and now there's a gap.

My counselor, my mentor, my leader, my friend,
  I'll long for your presence till my own end.
We have no choice in the length of our stay,
  So we must fulfill each and every day.

Our life with you was filled with love,
  But it's time to release you to our Lord above.
Now dear friend you must answer His call,
  You'll be with the Most Exalted of all.

So dear Chuck it's time to say,
  Good-bye until we meet again someday.
Go dearest friend, we'll not be sad,
  As we know you are in the arms of GOD!

Index

Index

Index